Kentucky

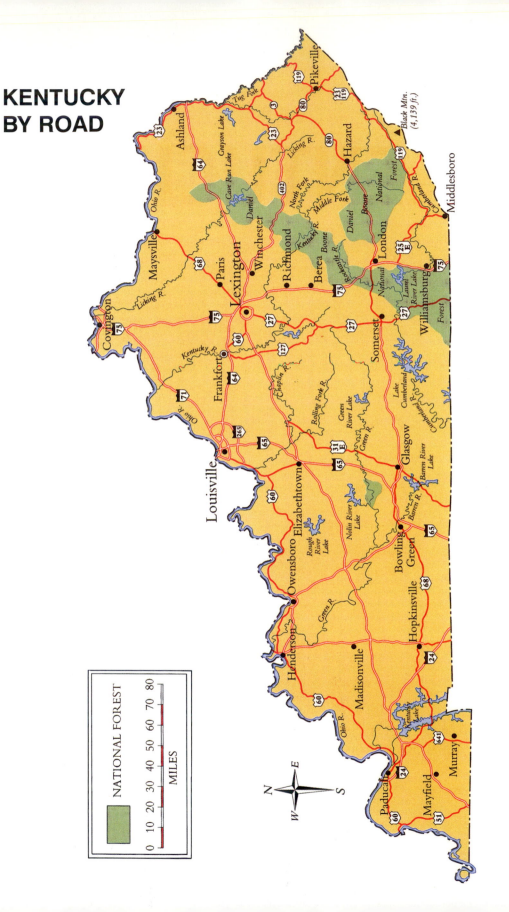

KENTUCKY BY ROAD

Celebrate the States

Kentucky

Tracy Barrett

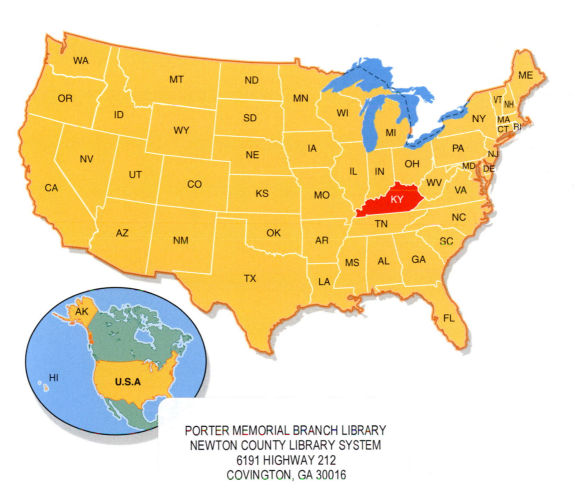

Marshall Cavendish
Benchmark
New York

Marshall Cavendish Benchmark
99 White Plains Road
Tarrytown, NY 10591-9001
www.marshallcavendish.us

All Internet addresses were correct and accurate at the time of printing.

Library of Congress Cataloging-in-Publication Data
Barrett, Tracy, 1955–
Kentucky / by Tracy Barrett. — 2nd ed.
p. cm. — (Celebrate the states)
Summary: "Provides comprehensive information on the geography, history, wildlife, governmental structure, economy, cultural diversity, peoples, religion, and landmarks of Kentucky"—Provided by publisher.
Includes bibliographical references and index.
ISBN 978-0-7614-2715-5
1. Kentucky—Juvenile literature. I. Title. II. Series.
F451.3.B37 2007
976.9—dc22
2007006388

Editor: Christine Florie
Publisher: Michelle Bisson
Art Director: Anahid Hamparian
Series Designer: Adam Mietlowski

Photo research by Connie Gardner

Cover photo by Kevin R. Morris/CORBIS

Alamy: Daniel Dempster, back cover; Jim Lane, 53; Wm. Baker/GhostWorx Images, 58, 92; *The Granger Collection:* 29, 66; *Corbis:* Kevin R. Morris, 8, 55, 65, 78, 111, 131; Mark E. Gibson, 14; David Muench, 15, 85, 137; Raymond Gehman, 17, 90; Ric Ergenbright, 18; Bettmann, 26, 35, 39, 41, 51, 57, 117; Underwood and Underwood, 37; Bill Luster, 42; John Atashian, 56; Corbis, 67; Marion Post Wolcott, 69; Bob Krist, 71; John Sommers II, 80; Kit Houghton, 81; Buddy Mays, 89; Layne Kennedy, 95; Richard Hamilton Smith 97 (bottom); W. Perry Conway, 101; Stapleton Collection, 115; Rufus E. Folks, 119, 123; Fred Prouser, 124; Deborah Feingold, 125; Owen Franken, 127; Anne Griffiths Belt, 135; *Getty:* Hulton Archive, 34; AFP, 11; Scott Goldsmith, 108; Stringer, 129; *AP Photo:* Debbie Caldwell, 63; Robert Bruck, 74; John Flavell, 76; *Gibson Stock Photography:* 88, 93; *PhotoEdit:* Dennis MacDonald, 72; *Dembinsky Photo Associates:* Dan Dempster, 12; Stephen J. Shaluta, Jr., 21; Skip Moody, 97 (TOP); Mark E. Gibson, 106; *Photo Researchers:* Dante Felonio, 16; Art Wolfe, 20; *The Image Works:* Fritz Poelking, 19; Moroney La Belle, 46, 133; Ann Ronan Picture Library, 49; Andre Jenny, 60; UPPA Topham, 113; *North Wind Picture Archive:* 22, 24, 32; *SuperStock:* agefotostock, 27, 82.

Printed in Malaysia
1 3 5 6 4 2

Contents

Kentucky Is . . .

Kentuckians are friendly . . .

"You know you're in Kentucky, because every door is open to a stranger."

—author Bobbie Ann Mason

. . . and they are strong and spirited.

"A Kentuckian kneels to none except his God, and always dies facing his enemy."

—Mexican War hero William Logan Crittenden, on refusing to kneel or wear a blindfold when executed in Cuba 1850

"Tough girls come from New York. Sweet girls, they're from Georgia. But us Kentucky girls, we have fire and ice in our blood. We can ride horses, be a debutante, [and] throw left hooks . . . all the while making sweet tea, darlin'. And if we have an opinion, you know you're gonna hear it."

—actress Ashley Judd

Kentuckians love their state . . .

"My vision for Kentucky is a Commonwealth where there is so much economic opportunity, and our quality of life is so high, that people who are born here can stay here, and people who aren't fortunate enough to be born in Kentucky, can look forward to locating here."

—Kentucky governor Ernie Fletcher (2003–2007)

"I saw a boomerang at a Louisville store that had 'Kentucky' printed across its face, and I thought, 'What a perfect metaphor.' So many of my friends left Kentucky as soon as we graduated [from] high school, and nearly all of us boomeranged back here once we had children of our own. It seems if your roots are here, they end up pulling you right back to the bluegrass."

—Kentuckian Darcy Maloney

"If these United States can be called a body, Kentucky can be called its heart."

—author Jesse Stuart

"If you like the outdoors, you'll love Kentucky. The state and national parks offer many great places to hike, camp, fish, and explore."

—Kentuckian Patricia Wiles

. . . and its beauty.

"Kentucky . . . [is] a second paradise."

—pioneer Daniel Boone

"Heaven is a Kentucky kind of place."

—Anonymous, 1700s

Some people think that the name "Kentucky" comes from a Native-American word meaning "dark and bloody ground." Although this is probably untrue, Kentucky has sometimes been a bloody place. From conflicts among different Native-American tribes to battles between settlers and Native Americans, the Civil War, the feuds of eastern Kentucky, the Black Patch War, and modern racial clashes, Kentucky has seen more than its share of violence. But Kentuckians have worked hard for peace, and their efforts are paying off. They now have a crime rate below the national average. Today, Kentucky is a busy and productive state, with one of the most innovative school systems in the country, thriving industry, and proud citizens. Come explore the Bluegrass State and see why its people have worked so hard to make the state a peaceful, as well as beautiful, place to live.

Chapter One

A Kentucky Kind of Place

Many things come to mind when someone mentions Kentucky. The Kentucky Derby. Fried chicken. Bluegrass. Kentucky is all these things and much more. But it's hard to pinpoint exactly what—or even where—Kentucky is.

Of course Kentucky can be found on a map. But is it in the South or the Midwest, or even in the North? People have different opinions about its location. It is not really in the South geographically. Most people in Kentucky identify themselves as Southerners, but Kentucky has characteristics of all the regions mentioned above.

Kentucky is one of the fifty states, but its official name is the "Commonwealth of Kentucky." In its beginning as part of the United States, Kentucky was just a portion of the Commonwealth of Virginia. Virginia calls itself a *commonwealth*, which in the colonial days was an alternative word for *state*. This explains why Kentucky—along with Massachusetts, Pennsylvania, and Virginia—is a commonwealth, although most people refer to all four locations as states.

Though not a large state, Kentucky has five geographic regions, one being the Bluegrass region (left).

Although the name "Kentucky" certainly comes from a Native-American word, no one is precisely sure which one and no one knows exactly what it means. It is most likely a Wyandot word, *Kentahteh*, meaning "land of tomorrow," or an Iroquois word, *Kentake*, meaning "meadow land."

Some people say that Kentucky is shaped like a dented shield. Others think that it looks like a camel lying down. Kentucky's southern border is flat, and its northern edge rises to a jagged peak, just like one of the mountains in the state's eastern section. At Kentucky's peak, near the center of the state, it measures 180 miles north to south, while in the west, it narrows to a mere 40 miles.

Kentucky is bordered on the north by Ohio, Indiana, and Illinois; on the west by Missouri; on the south by Tennessee; and on the east by Virginia and West Virginia. One part of Kentucky cannot be reached by land except from another state: 18 square miles that lie inside a loop of the Mississippi River must be entered from Tennessee.

THE BIRTH OF KENTUCKY

Hundreds of millions of years ago an ocean covered what is now Kentucky. The Appalachian Mountains began rising out of this ocean 230 million years ago, as large plates of land pushed slowly against each other and crumpled into mountains. Toward the west, the plates sloped off into what is now flat farmland. In the eastern part of the state, the broken edges of the plates gradually wore away into odd rounded hills that are now called the Knobs. After the mountains rose and the ocean poured into what is now the Atlantic, huge, swampy forests grew. The enormous coal deposits in eastern Kentucky are the remnants of this forest. Even after two centuries of mining, about 85 to 88 billion tons of coal remain in the ground there.

Coal deposits in eastern Kentucky were formed from decomposing ancient forests.

Although the swamps are long gone, Kentucky is still a green state. The Bluegrass region is named for the grass that covers the central part of the state. There, large horse farms spread across gentle hills. Louisville, the state's largest city, sits on the bank of the Ohio River. South-central Kentucky is filled with fertile farmland, fascinating caves, and lovely lakes. As the state flattens away to the west, the landscape opens up.

Pastureland thrives in the fertile soil of the Bluegrass region.

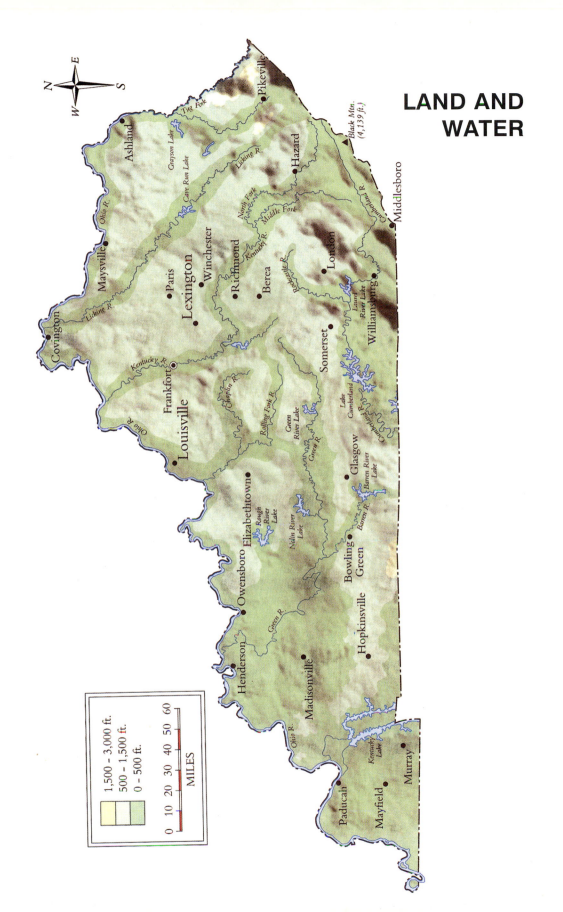

LAND AND WATER

Black Mtn.
(4,139 ft.)

Pikeville

Tug Fork

Ashland

Grayson Lake

Cave Run Lake

Licking R.

Hazard

Ohio R.

North Fork

Middle Fork

Cumberland R.

Middlesboro

Maysville

Winchester

Paris

Lexington

Richmond

Berea

Kentucky R.

Redbird R.

London

Laurel River Lake

Williamsburg

Covington

Licking R.

Kentucky R.

Frankfort

Chaplin R.

Somerset

Lake Cumberland

Louisville

Ohio R.

Rolling Fork R.

Green River Lake

Green R.

Cumberland R.

Elizabethtown

Owensboro

Rough River Lake

Nolin River Lake

Glasgow

Barren River Lake

Barren R.

Bowling Green

Green R.

Henderson

Hopkinsville

Madisonville

Ohio R.

Kentucky Lake

Murray

Paducah

Mayfield

Scale

1,500 – 3,000 ft.
500 – 1,500 ft.
0 – 500 ft.

MILES

0   10   20   30   40   50   60

WATER AND WEATHER

Kentucky is watered by 13,000 miles of streams and rivers. Among the fifty states, only Alaska has more miles of running water. The mighty Ohio River, which runs along Kentucky's northern border, is wide and calm. Most of Kentucky's major cities, such as Louisville, Owensboro, Covington, and Paducah, grew up along the easily navigated Ohio.

But many of the state's smaller streams rush down hillsides and through narrow gorges. "This is a great state for white-water," says enthusiastic visitor Greg Giles. "If you like exciting rapids, you can find them, or you can paddle a canoe down a quiet stream. They have some of everything here." At the bottom of Kentucky's rivers you can sometimes find geodes, round rocks that when cracked open reveal "a whole crystal world," recalls former Kentuckian Miriam Moore.

A tributary of the Mississippi River, the Ohio River flows along the Louisville shores.

Many of Kentucky's rivers are fed by underground streams. These streams have carved out at least two thousand caves, the most of any state in the country. Kentucky's Mammoth Cave is the largest known cave system in the world, but most of the state's caves are small. Still, Kentuckians have taken advantage of them. Milbrey Dugger's grandfather lived on a farm near Cave City during the Civil War. "Pappa told me that during the war, soldiers would sweep

At 350 miles long and 379 feet deep, central Kentucky's Mammoth Cave is the largest in the world.

through the countryside and steal everything they could find," she recalls. "The children were posted as lookouts, and whenever they heard of any soldiers in the area, they would take the cattle and horses into the caves and hide them there until the coast was clear."

Caves keep to a constant temperature, but in Kentucky as a whole, the temperature in winter often drops below freezing, while summers are hot and humid, especially in low-lying areas. Becky Ray, who grew up on a farm near Louisville in the 1950s, remembers the summer heat as being unbearable in her old house, which had a tin roof. "We had no electricity or running water," she recalls. "But it was so hot that we got electricity first so we could have an air conditioner even before we had water in the house." Kentucky averages 48 inches of rain each year, but in some years the rain is so heavy that it combines with the many rivers and streams in the state and causes dangerous floods. Flash floods caused severe damage in 1997, and in 2002 more flooding caused the governor to declare a state of emergency in twelve counties. Snow falls throughout the state, with the mountains receiving the most, usually about 15 inches each winter.

THE ENDANGERED BAT

Kentucky's intriguing caves attract throngs of visitors each year. At first glance these caves may seem deserted, but in truth they are home to many varieties of wildlife. One of these is the gray bat.

Bats are shy creatures. They do not fly into people's hair or attack visitors in their caves. Instead of posing a threat, bats are actually affected by their human visitors. As visitors flood into caves, the bats' roosting areas are disturbed. Some bats stop reproducing or abandon their babies when people come too close. Also, pesticide use and land development have changed the caves' environment and reduced the population of the insects the bats prey on.

All of these factors have combined to put the gray bat on the Endangered Species list. Cave visitors are encouraged to be careful around the bats' roosting sites and to keep out of the caves while the bats are there. In some areas the placement of fences at cave entrances has helped restore the gray bat population.

KENTUCKY WILDLIFE

Because Kentucky has both mountains and plains, a large variety of plants and animals live there. Thick forests, which cover half the state, are full of hardwood trees, such as ash, hickory, maple, and oak, as well as softwoods, such as cypress, hemlock, and pine. A tremendous assortment of trees thrives in Kentucky—in all, 175 species, including eleven varieties of oak alone. "There are many kinds of nut trees in Kentucky," says Miriam Moore, who grew up in southeastern Kentucky. "And anyone who knows where to look can have a snack just for the picking." As children, Miriam and her friends were given strict instructions to stay on the paths while exploring the woods because the trees were so thick that losing sight of the trail after just a few steps was very easy to do.

The smallest-known flowering plant in the world lives in Kentucky. This plant, the watermeal, is no larger than a pinhead and produces microscopic flowers. Kentucky is also home to goldenrod, azaleas, buttercups, mountain laurel, and rhododendrons. In the springtime these flowering plants splash color across hills and meadows. The most famous plant in Kentucky, the one that gave the state its nickname, is not native to the Americas. Bluegrass was brought to the area by English settlers. It has spread over most of central Kentucky, and for much of the year looks like regular grass. But in the spring its new blades turn the hills of central Kentucky a soft blue-green color.

Kentucky's forestland covers more than 11 million acres. That's almost half the state!

Bluegrass is a thick and healthy grass that varies in color depending on the season.

More than three hundred species of birds grace Kentucky's skies. The largest and most spectacular are bald eagles, hawks, and ospreys. Once extinct in the state, wild turkeys have been reintroduced and are now thriving, while owls hunt in the woods there at night. They are joined by many mammals. The largest are black bear and white-tailed deer. Coyotes are occasionally seen, and skunks, mice, shrews, and river otters abound. Raccoons, squirrels, possums, and other small mammals thrive in the mild climate. Naturally, with so much water, lots of fish live in Kentucky. You will find many Kentuckians down by their favorite stream, casting for bass, walleye, sucker, crappie, rainbow trout, and sauger.

Ospreys use their feet to grab their prey in the lakes and streams of Kentucky.

Kentucky's wildlife used to be even more diverse than it is today. Some of the earliest animals—mastodons, woolly mammoth, big-horned bison, giant armadillos, and giant sloths—became extinct as the climate changed. Later, early white and black settlers drove away or killed such animals as elk, cougars, and wolves. In the eighteenth century Kentucky had 18 million acres of forest, 2 million acres of prairie, and 1.6 million acres of wetlands. Today, the forests have shrunk to 11.9 million acres. No prairies remain, and the wetlands have shrunk to less than half their former size. Some of the animals that called the forests, prairies, and wetlands home have also disappeared.

Large herds of elk used to roam the forests and plains of Kentucky, but they had been extinct for almost two hundred years before being reintroduced into the state in 1997. They prospered, and in 2006 the herd was estimated to number 5,700, the largest in the eastern United States.

Kentucky's elk population is expected to grow due to the lack of natural predators.

Some trees that were once common in Kentucky's forests are now scarce. Many of Kentucky's beautiful chestnut trees were destroyed in a blight that spread across North America during the early twentieth century. The majestic elms that grew to towering heights were almost totally wiped out by Dutch elm disease, caused by a fungus that was introduced to North America in 1931. Most of the state's huge, ancient oaks were felled for lumber. While oaks still grow in Kentucky, very few of them approach the height or girth of their ancestors. In fact, most trees in Kentucky's forests today are smaller than those of a few centuries ago.

Recently, some trees in Kentucky have become covered by thick vines called kudzu that gradually choke the life out of them. The broad leaves of the vines keep sunlight from reaching the trees they cover. Kudzu is grown in Japan as food for both people and cattle and was introduced into the American South as a decorative plant. But because it has no natural predators in Kentucky, it has grown out of control.

People try to cut it down, but it grows so fast that many give up. "If you sit and watch it for a few minutes, you can actually see it grow," says frustrated farmer Kathy Simpson. "Since it grows where your cattle graze, you don't want to use a strong herbicide on it and poison the animals. I suppose I'll have to learn to live with it."

Kentucky's history is filled with stories of men and women surviving despite many obstacles and hardships. This same perseverance and resourcefulness should help Kentuckians as they grapple with the challenges of protecting their state's lovely countryside.

Fast-growing kudzu spreads over everything, even telephone poles.

Chapter Two

Yesterday and Today

The first humans to arrive in what is now Kentucky followed mastodons and other large animals into the area 12,000 years ago. These prehistoric people probably did not stay long in any one place.

THE FIRST KENTUCKIANS

About 10,000 years later, people of what anthropologists now call the Adena culture settled in north-central Kentucky. They established villages, mostly along rivers, and planted crops. They lived in houses made of wood and dried mud and buried their dead in huge mounds, some of which can still be seen. No one knows where the Adena Indians went; perhaps they moved on to another place, or maybe they stayed and merged with the next group of people to arrive, now called the Hopewell Indians. The Hopewell developed extensive trade networks with peoples as far away as present-day Michigan.

EUROPEAN EXPLORERS

English explorers had first come through the area in the mid-1600s, and the Frenchman René-Robert Cavelier, Sieur de La Salle, may have explored

New immigrants and settlers from the east traveled over Kentucky's rough terrain in hope of owning their own land.

the region in his travels between 1669 and 1671. By this time Kentucky was no longer the permanent home of any Native-American tribe. It was used as a kind of game preserve, where members of many different tribes, including the Shawnees, Cherokees, Chickasaws, Wyandots, Delawares, Yuchis, and Iroquois, would hunt. The abundant game and fertile land was also attracting droves of European settlers. For the most part, these groups had few conflicts. But eventually that changed. During the seventeenth and eighteenth centuries, the Iroquois traded animal skins to Dutch colonists in exchange for guns, and then chased out many of their rivals.

Some Shawnees resisted Iroquois aggression. By canoe and foot the Shawnees could reach the Great Lakes, the Atlantic Ocean, and the Gulf of Mexico. Game was plentiful. They had no intention of moving to a less comfortable place, and they struggled fiercely to keep their land, which was being settled by both blacks and whites. In 1774 several different Native-American tribes, especially the Shawnee, united to try to drive the settlers back across the Appalachian Mountains. Lord Dunsmore, the governor of Virginia, sent troops to help

Native Americans hunted deer by moonlight in the region that is now Kentucky.

the settlers, and after five months of fighting, the colonist forces were successful. The Shawnee and their allies had to give up much of their land and agree not to attack settlers anymore.

THE PLEIADES AND THE PINE: A CHEROKEE TALE

One day seven young boys were playing ball when they were supposed to be working. Their mothers scolded them, and the boys ran off into the woods to the spot where dances were held.

They started dancing around and around. They danced for so long that their mothers got worried and came to look for them. As their mothers drew near, they saw the boys dancing. But as they watched, the boys' feet began rising off the earth. The women ran to grab their sons, but it was too late—the boys were floating high above their reach. One mother made a great leap, seized her son's foot, and pulled him to the ground. But she had pulled too hard, and her son hit the ground with such force that he sank into it and disappeared from sight.

The other six boys continued dancing and rising as their weeping mothers called to them. They finally ascended into the sky and became the constellation Ani'tsutsä (the Boys), which is also known as the Pleiades. The mother whose son had plunged into the earth came to cry over him every day until a green plant grew up out of the soil where he lay. It eventually became the tall tree called the pine, which the Cherokees say has the same nature as the stars.

THE FRONTIER PASSES BY

Exploring Kentucky was difficult. Its woods were so thick that it was hard to take more than a few steps without brushing against a branch, tripping over a root, or getting hemmed in by shrubbery. Add to this the oppressive heat and humidity and the mountainous, rocky terrain, and many modern travelers would feel like giving up after a short walk. It is little wonder that when people left their homes in the East for the wilds of Kentucky, their families often held funerals for them.

Thomas Walker, a doctor from Virginia, aided exploration of the region immensely when he found a low spot in the mountains in 1750. The Cumberland Gap, as he called this pass, soon became the most important route to the West. The famed historian Frederick Jackson Turner once wrote, "Stand at Cumberland Gap and watch the procession of civilization, marching single file—the buffalo following the trail to the salt springs, the Indian, the fur-trader and hunter, the cattle-raiser, the pioneer farmer—and the frontier has passed by."

Fabled explorer Daniel Boone made his first trip through the Cumberland Gap in 1767, and in 1775 he helped blaze a trail, the Wilderness Road, through Kentucky's forests. Boone's exploring skills were legendary, and he himself once said that he had never gotten lost, exactly, but was "bewildered once for three days." His Wilderness Road became the major trail westward for pioneers.

In 1775 Daniel Boone led settlers through the Cumberland Gap, which was part of the Wilderness Road—a route to the West.

THE GROWTH OF A STATE

In 1774 Virginia's Governor Dunsmore sent James Harrod to explore Kentucky. He led a group of colonists through the Cumberland Gap and founded Harrodsburg, Kentucky's first permanent non-Native settlement. A year later Daniel Boone established a fort at a site his followers called Boonesborough.

After the American colonies declared their independence from Britain in 1776, those loyal to the crown encouraged Native Americans to attack settlers whenever possible. Boonesborough was one of the towns attacked. Early settlers often took refuge in Boone's fort during these attacks.

Fort Boonesborough provided shelter and safety to settlers traveling west on the Wilderness Road.

At the end of the American Revolution in 1783, the area that later became Kentucky had a population of only about 12,000 and was still part of the Commonwealth of Virginia. Between 1775 and 1795 more than 100,000 people poured through the Cumberland Gap. Some continued to head west, but many remained in Kentucky to take advantage of the fertile farmland and abundant hunting. By 1790 Kentucky's population had boomed to more than 70,000, and two years later Kentucky became the fifteenth state.

A LITTLE HERO

In 1791 a group of settlers traveling down the Ohio River was attacked by Indians. Three of the nine men in the party were killed and four were seriously wounded. One of the survivors wrote:

The women and children were all uninjured excepting a little son of Mr. Plascut, who after the battle was over, came to the Captain, and with great coolness, requested him to take a ball [bullet] out of his head. On examination it appeared that a ball that had passed through the side of the boat, had penetrated the forehead of this little hero and remained under the skin. The Captain took it out, when the lad observed, "that is not all," raised his arm and exhibited a piece of bone at the point of his elbow, which had been shot off and hung by the skin. His mother exclaimed, "why did you not tell me of this?" "Because," he coolly replied, "the Captain directed us to be silent during the action, and I thought you would be likely to make a noise if I told you."

Because of the rich farmland, especially in the Bluegrass region, agriculture quickly became the most important source of income in the state. After the steamboat was invented in the late eighteenth century, agricultural products could be more easily shipped to other parts of the country. Kentucky thrived, as its farmers sold huge quantities of hemp, corn, tobacco, wheat, and flax.

BLACK AND WHITE IN KENTUCKY

Most crops were raised at least in part by slave labor. Black Americans had been in Kentucky as long as white settlers. By 1830 slaves never made up more than 24 percent of Kentucky's population. Although this number may seem large, in the Deep South, more than half the population was in slavery. Most enslaved Kentuckians labored in fields, while some worked in mining and manufacturing.

Kentucky's farms were generally smaller than those in the other slave states. Most slaveholding farmers in Kentucky owned fewer than five slaves. When a slaveholder sold his slaves, families were frequently split up.

Steamboats line the Louisville port, waiting to transport cargo and passengers along the Ohio River.

THE HUNTERS OF KENTUCKY

Frontier bragging was very much an accepted form of expression. Andrew Jackson's Kentucky riflemen let it be known that they were "half a horse and half an alligator." This song details their exploits against the British at the Battle of New Orleans, January 8, 1815. It was later used as a campaign song for Jackson in the presidential election of 1824.

We are a hardy, free-born race,
Each man to fear a stranger;
Whate'er the game we join in chase,
Despoiling time and danger;
And if a daring foe annoys
Whate'er his strength and forces,
We'll show him that Kentucky boys
Are alligator horses. *Chorus*

I s'pose you've read it in the prints,
How Packenham attempted
To make old Hickory Jackson wince,
But soon his scheme repented;
For we, with rifles ready cocked,
Thought such occasion lucky,
And soon around the gen'ral flocked
The hunters of Kentucky. *Chorus*

So Packenham he made his brags,
If he in fight was lucky,
He'd have their girls and cotton bags,
In spite of old Kentucky. *Chorus*

But Jackson, he was wide awake,
And was not scared of trifles;
For well he knew what aim we take
With our Kentucky rifles;
He led us down to Cypress Swamp,
the ground was low and mucky;
There stood John Bull in pomp,
And here was old Kentucky. *Chorus*

A bank was raised to hide our breasts,
Not that we thought of dying,
But that we always like to rest,
Unless the game is flying;
Behind it stood out a little force,
None wished it to be greater,
For every man was half a horse
And half an alligator. *Chorus*

They did not let our patience tire,
Before they showed their faces;
We did not choose to waste our fire
So snugly kept our places;
But when so near we saw them wink,
We thought it time to stop 'em,
And 'twould have done you good, I think,
To see Kentuckians drop 'em. *Chorus*

They found, at last, 'twas vain to fight,
Where lead was all the booty,
And so they widely took to flight,
And left us all our beauty;
And now, if danger e'er annoys,
Remember what our trade is,
Just send for us Kentucky boys,
And we'll protect ye, ladies. *Chorus*

Black Kentuckians, both slave and free, were treated quite differently from whites. There were four crimes for which a white person could be executed, while eleven crimes were considered severe enough to execute a black person.

A SLAVE AUCTION

Isaac Johnson's mother was a slave and his father was a slave owner. His father sold his family when he was eleven years old. He later wrote:

I was [sold] for seven hundred dollars . . . to William Madinglay, who came forward and said: "Come along with me, boy, you belong to me." I said to him: "Let me go and see my mother." He answered me crossly: "Come along with me, I will train you without your mother's help." I was taken to one side and chained to a post as though I had been a horse. . . .

The next to be set up was my mother. . . .

The next sale was of Eddie, my little brother, whom we all loved so much, he was sold for two hundred dollars. . . . Thus, in a very short time, our happy family was scattered, without even the privilege of saying "Good by" [sic] to each other, and never again to be seen, at least so far as I was concerned.

Most of the time, slaves had no choice but to put up with their miserable conditions. But in a few cases slaves took matters into their own hands. In the most famous slave uprising in Kentucky, in August 1818, between fifty-five and seventy-five slaves armed themselves and tried to escape to freedom. They got into a gun battle with the state militia, and most were captured.

But some white Kentuckians were more forceful than the rest in their refusal to accept the poor treatment of blacks. For example, before the Civil War, Berea College was founded with the aim of providing a college education to anyone who wanted one, whatever the student's race, religion, or ability to pay.

A STATE DIVIDED

Throughout the first half of the nineteenth century, the right of individual states to make their own laws, including deciding whether slavery would be legal, was hotly debated between the North and the South. Kentucky was torn. On the one hand, Kentucky had passed a law in 1833 forbidding anyone to bring slaves into the state for resale. On the other hand, most Kentuckians had come from the Southern slaveholding states and were accustomed to the practice.

When eleven other slaveholding states seceded from the Union and formed the Confederate States of America, Kentucky decided to stay with the Union. But Kentuckians remained divided in their loyalty. During the Civil War some 35,000 Kentuckians fought for the Confederacy, while about 90,000 fought for the Union. Both sides included a star on their flags to represent Kentucky.

The war divided not only the state, but also towns and even families. Former Kentucky governor John J. Crittendon had two sons. One became a general in the Confederate army, and the other a general in the Union army.

Both Abraham Lincoln, president of the United States during the Civil War, and Jefferson Davis, president of the Confederate States of America, were born in Kentucky.

Early in the war Kentuckian George R. Browder wrote in his diary, "I think we will have dark days in [Kentucky], & it will be long perhaps before the war is over." He was right.

No extended Civil War battles took place in Kentucky. The Battle of Perryville, in October 1862, was the bloodiest, with 7,500 soldiers killed or wounded. But during the war the state was overrun by guerrillas fighting small skirmishes and raiding and burning down homes. Many farms were damaged or destroyed. Some Kentuckians, despairing of ever being able to make a living from agriculture again, turned to manufacturing. When the war ended in 1865, Kentucky found itself in desperate shape. Not only were its farms in ruins, but the cities that had bought the state's produce had

The Battle of Mills Spring was the second-largest Civil War battle to take place in Kentucky.

also been devastated by the war and could no longer buy much, further weakening the economy.

Although civil rights were granted to Kentucky's blacks in 1865, relations between blacks and whites remained tense. In the fifteen years following the war, almost 150 blacks were executed by a mob, or lynched. Public education for Kentucky's blacks was established, but there was so little funding that few actually attended school.

COAL AND TOBACCO

After the Civil War the nation and the world became more dependent on manufacturing, increasing the demand for coal. Coal was also used to fuel the railroads, which were expanding rapidly at this time. Because Kentucky had a large coal supply, its economy began to revive from the horrors of the war.

The development of hardier strains of tobacco, which grew well in Kentucky, was also a boon to the state's economy. Tobacco production in Kentucky tripled between 1870 and 1900, and it became the state's most important crop.

Realizing how profitable tobacco was, some growers banded together to try to raise the price paid for tobacco in the region.

Tobacco was (and often still is) sold at auctions (above).

Some farmers resisted joining these cooperatives. The result was several years of violence in the so-called Black Patch War, which was named for the dark leaves of one kind of tobacco. Between 1905 and 1909, night riders, who called themselves Possum Hunters, terrorized the farmers who refused to band together. They burned farms, destroyed fields, and whipped and murdered their opponents. After years of violence, the conflict finally died down with neither side declaring victory.

In 1917 the United States entered World War I. By war's end 80,000 Kentuckians had served in the armed forces. In Breathitt County not a single man had to be drafted because so many eligible men signed up voluntarily. This was the only county in the entire country where the draft was not necessary.

World War I caused a huge increase in the need for coal, bringing prosperity to Kentucky. Many farmers sold their land and went to work in the mines. But when the war ended, so did the great demand for coal. With no farms to return to, many Kentuckians went broke.

Those who still had jobs in the mines were hardly better off. Not only was the work dirty and dangerous, but the miners were also poorly paid. Most lived in towns built by the mining companies and bought their goods at high prices in stores the companies owned as well. The miners and the mine owners clashed frequently, and often violently. Harlan County, the scene of much of the fighting, was called Bloody Harlan.

During the Great Depression of the 1930s, when the U.S. economy went into a tailspin, Kentucky suffered along with the rest of the country. Farmers and miners had few reserves to fall back on, and when banks failed to make farm loans and coal mines closed down, the workers had few skills that would enable them to transfer to new jobs. The government tried to help by constructing power plants and phone lines, which

Before machinery was used in mining, miners had the difficult and dangerous job of cutting coal with picks and shovels.

brought electricity and telephone service to much of the state, in many cases for the first time. Roads and schools were also improved. Kentucky's economy didn't really rebound until the beginning of World War II, which again increased the demand for coal.

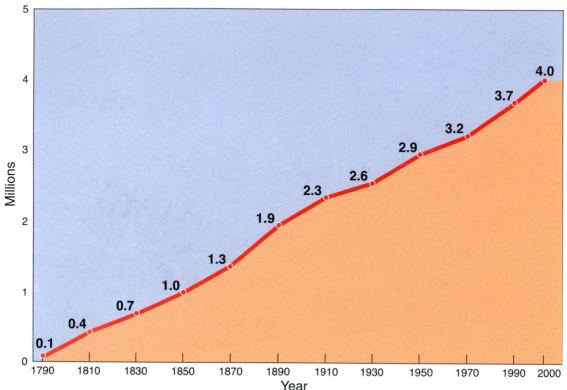

POPULATION GROWTH: 1790–2000

Millions / Year

0.1, 0.4, 0.7, 1.0, 1.3, 1.9, 2.3, 2.6, 2.9, 3.2, 3.7, 4.0

TO THE PRESENT

In the years after the war, some Kentuckians turned their attention to the injustices suffered by the state's black citizens. For decades blacks had been forced to attend separate schools from whites, and they endured widespread discrimination in all walks of life.

But gradually legal discrimination began to be stripped away. In the mid-1950s Louisville became the first large southern city to admit blacks to schools that had previously only allowed whites. Although some white Kentuckians resisted it, this integration of the public schools was more peaceful than it would be in the coming years in many other states.

African-American and white students peacefully enter a school in mid-1950s Louisville.

In 1964 civil rights leader Martin Luther King Jr. led a march in Frankfort to encourage the passage of a civil rights law. Although this bill did not pass, two years later Kentucky became the first southern state to enact such a law, which King described as "the strongest and most comprehensive civil rights bill passed by a southern state."

Civil rights were slow to come to the state, but many Kentuckians helped speed up the process. Kentucky's Young family produced many remarkable civil rights advocates. Whitney Moore Young Sr. was once the head of the department of engineering at the then all-black Lincoln Institute. He was later promoted to dean and education director of the school. He was twice president of Kentucky's Negro Education Association and in 1964 was appointed by President Lyndon Johnson to oversee the implementation of civil rights laws. His son Whitney Moore Young Jr. was head of the National Urban League from 1961 until his death in 1971. He was a nationally recognized leader of the civil rights movement and helped open up many jobs and educational opportunities for African Americans. His sister Anita Young was one of the first African-American deans at the University of Louisville.

The history and culture of Kentucky's Native-American citizens is being recognized today more than in the past. In 2004 the Kentucky Native American Commission was formed with the goal that "all Kentuckians will recognize, appreciate and understand the significant contributions Native Americans have made to Kentucky's rich cultural heritage. Through education and increased awareness, the people of Kentucky will understand the histories, cultures and matters of concern to Native American peoples." Part of the commission's mission is to teach about and communicate the rich diversity and heritage of Native-American peoples in Kentucky.

Whitney Moore Young Jr. (left) meets with President Lyndon B. Johnson to discuss African-American unemployment.

Kentuckians have worked hard to make their state a good place to live. They have a proud tradition to draw on. Author Wendell Berry once wrote that in Kentucky forests one can feel the presence of "the ancient tribesmen who used to inhabit the rock houses of the cliffs; of the white hunters from east of the mountains; of the farmers who accepted the isolation of these nearly inaccessible valleys. . . . If one spends much time here and feels much liking for the place, it is hard to escape the sense of one's predecessors." Many Kentuckians would be quick to agree as they strive to live up to their state's great heritage.

Chapter Three

Proud People

Almost all Kentuckians were born in the United States, and most of them were born in Kentucky. With the lovely countryside, thriving cities, and fascinating past, why would they want to live anywhere else? Kentuckians prove their love for their state by living out their lives where they were born.

A RURAL PAST

Kentuckians have always been drawn to the state's beautiful countryside. But the steep hills and narrow valleys make road construction difficult, so in the past Kentuckians who didn't live in major cities were often quite isolated. In the 1960s most Kentuckians lived in the country rather than in cities and towns. Even today, only a little more than half the state's population is found in cities. Nationally, the proportion of city dwellers is closer to three-quarters.

Kentucky pride abounds, even in the state's youngest residents.

POPULATION DENSITY

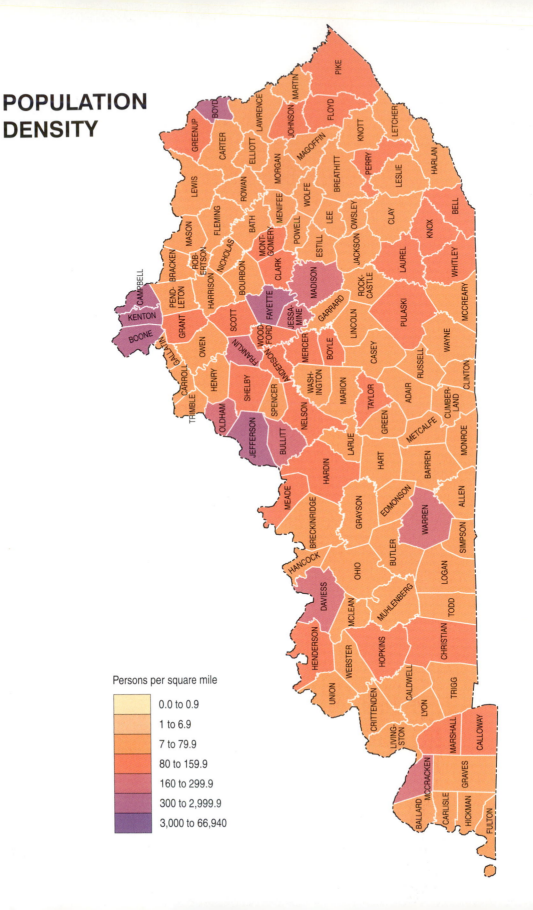

Persons per square mile

- 0.0 to 0.9
- 1 to 6.9
- 7 to 79.9
- 80 to 159.9
- 160 to 299.9
- 300 to 2,999.9
- 3,000 to 66,940

Although Kentucky has grown more urban and prosperous in recent years, Kentuckians honor their diligent forebears, who had to scrape their living off the land, in such events as the International Bar-B-Q Festival in Owensboro. Some of the meat barbecued at this event is mutton—the meat from sheep—because sheep could thrive on even the state's most rugged, rocky terrain, which has only sparse vegetation, and cattle had a harder time finding enough to eat. Aside from barbecue tastings and cook-offs, festival visitors are treated to a crafts fair, a fiddling contest, dancing, and a pie-eating contest.

Kentucky also boasts its own traditional stew called burgoo. Each cook prepares burgoo in a different way, but all agree that it must have a lot of ingredients, since the dish was originally made from the contributions of many people, with each person adding something different to the pot. Traditionalists insist that burgoo must include wild game, such as squirrel meat, but nowadays cooks are more likely to use mutton, beef, or chicken.

LIVING TOGETHER

Seventy-two percent of Kentuckians were born in Kentucky, one of the highest proportions in the country. Fewer than 1 percent were born in a different country. The population of Kentucky in 2006 was just over four million people. Most Kentuckians—89 percent—are of European descent, primarily English, German, Irish, and Scottish. African Americans make up about 7 percent of the population, while Native Americans comprise 0.2 percent and Hispanics 2 percent. Asians and other groups each account for 1 percent.

Race relations in the state have long been troubled, but many think the situation is improving. Mary Anderson, a white woman who has

Many cultures and heritages are celebrated in Kentucky.

lived in Kentucky for all of her seventy-nine years, says, "Races are being accepted now more than they used to be. Integration may be slow, but it's coming. Many other races—not just blacks—are coming in: Hispanics, Arabs, Haitians. They are coming in from troubled spots all over the world."

KENTUCKY HOT BROWN

This dish named for Louisville's Brown Hotel, where it was first made, is a lunchtime favorite. Have an adult help you with this recipe.

    2 tablespoons butter
    2 tablespoons flour
    1 cup hot milk
    Salt and pepper to taste
    1/2 cup grated cheddar or American cheese
    1/2 teaspoon Worcestershire sauce
    8 slices bacon
    1 pound sliced turkey breast
    4 slices white toast
    2 tablespoons grated Parmesan
    8 pimento strips, canned

To make the sauce, melt the butter in a medium-size sauce pan. Add the flour and stir for one minute over low heat. Pour in the hot milk and whisk until smooth and thickened. Add salt and pepper. Remove from heat, then add the cheese and the Worcestershire sauce.

Meanwhile, grill the bacon in a pan.

On each piece of toast, arrange 1/4 pound of the turkey breast slices. Spread the sauce over the toast and turkey. Top with grated Parmesan and crisscrosses of bacon slices and pimiento. Broil until bubbling. Enjoy!

ETHNIC KENTUCKY

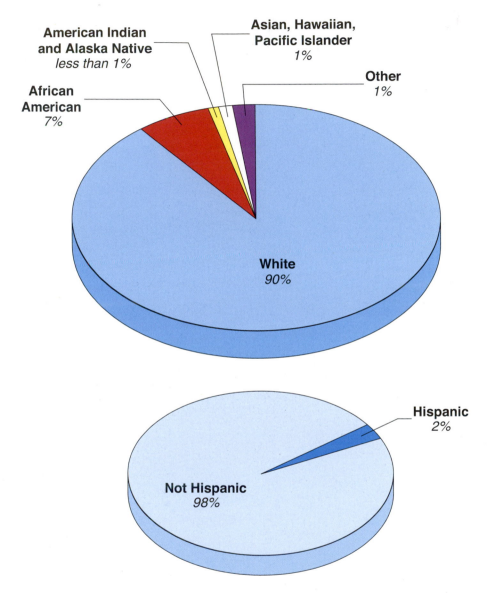

American Indian and Alaska Native
less than 1%

Asian, Hawaiian, Pacific Islander
1%

Other
1%

African American
7%

White
90%

Hispanic
2%

Not Hispanic
98%

Note: A person of Cuban, Mexican, Puerto Rican, South or Central American, or other Spanish culture or origin, regardless of race, is defined as Hispanic.

RELIGION

Most Kentuckians identify themselves as Protestant, with Baptists accounting for nearly half of the total church membership. Baptists have been in Kentucky for more than two centuries, and many of them belong to small sects with names like Old Regular Baptists, Primitive Baptists, and Free Will Baptists.

One of the most interesting religious groups that made a home in Kentucky was the Society of Believers, who are often called Shakers because of the rhythmic dances that formed part of their services. Shakers believed in living simply, worshiping God through work, and always striving to be perfect. In nineteenth-century Kentucky Shakers had two main settlements: Pleasant Hill near Harrodsburg and South Union near Bowling Green. In the 1850s there were about five thousand Shakers in the United States. But since their religion forbade them to marry and have children, the only way for the sect to grow was by recruiting new members. Very few Shakers remain today in the United States.

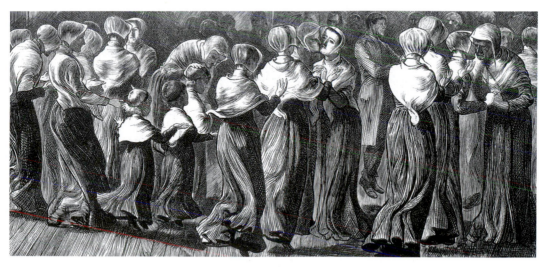

During services, Shakers dance with their palms facing upward to catch God's grace and blessing.

"THE DARK AND BLOODY GROUND"

Kentucky was once thought to be one of the most violent places in the United States. There are many possible reasons for this reputation. Throughout the nineteenth century many Kentuckians lived in isolated communities, far from the law, and had to make their own justice. Sometimes this meant that the most powerful person or family in a hamlet ruled the town and decided what punishment was appropriate for what crime. Also, Kentuckians had a high rate of alcohol consumption, which often led to violent fights. Many carried weapons, so minor quarrels sometimes escalated into gunfights. In the nineteenth century differences of opinion over whether Kentucky should join the Union or the Confederacy also led to tension between families and towns.

Pioneer Kentucky was a rough place. Until 1799, when the first prison was built, all serious crimes were punished by death since there were no facilities for holding prisoners. A lot has changed since then. Today, Kentucky has an extensive court system, and this once-violent state has a crime control record to be proud of. In 2005 Kentucky ranked ninth of all fifty states in its violent-crime rate.

Many people think of feuds when Kentucky is mentioned. A feud is a violent quarrel that goes on for years or even generations. It often starts when a member of one group injures a person from another group, and someone from the injured person's side seeks revenge. Then the first side avenges that injury, and so on, for years and years. From the mid-nineteenth to the early twentieth century, Kentucky's feuding families received much attention in the newspapers. The press usually ignored the real reasons for the disagreements, which often originated in local economic or political struggles, and made it sound as though the "hillbillies" just enjoyed shooting each other for no reason.

THE HATFIELDS AND THE MCCOYS

Although not the nation's bloodiest feud, the conflict between the Kentucky McCoys and the West Virginia Hatfields is the best known. Until the 1860s the two families lived in harmony. But then things changed, probably when a dead Union soldier from the McCoy family was found near the home of the pro-Confederacy Hatfields. The McCoys killed a Hatfield in revenge, and the feud took off.

In 1882 a Hatfield was murdered by three McCoys. The McCoys were caught, tied to a bush, and told by their Hatfield captors, "Boys, if you have any peace to make with your Maker you had better make it." Then, in the dim light of a lantern, they were shot.

The leader of the Hatfield clan, "Devil Anse" Hatfield, once said, "If you like, you can say it is the devil's Church that I belong to." The McCoy leader, Randolph McCoy, said that no neighbor of the Hatfields could doubt the existence of the devil.

By the time the feud subsided in 1891, somewhere between twelve and sixty-five people had been killed.

The feuds did not end in the nineteenth century. Miriam Moore says that during her childhood, before city dwellers would go to the top of the ridge behind her town, where the more traditional country people lived, they would check with the storekeeper to see if it was safe. "If someone was feuding, he'd tell them to keep out," she says.

KENTUCKY AT PLAY

People interested in old English, Scottish, and Irish customs love to visit Kentucky. "People are crazy about the Scottish games here," says Mary Jacobs, a Kentuckian of Scottish descent. "When the men dress up in kilts and the bagpipes start to play, you could imagine you were in cold, gray Scotland instead of hot, sunny Kentucky!"

When people arrived from the British Isles in the eighteenth and nineteenth centuries, they brought their folk songs, dances, musical instruments, and stories with them. While many of these customs have changed or disappeared in Europe, in the hills of Kentucky they are still alive, and in many ways have changed little in the last century or two.

Set dancing, a form of folk dance, is still popular in Kentucky. Some dances are from the sixteenth century, while others probably go back to the Middle Ages. These dances are sometimes accompanied by the Appalachian dulcimer, a stringed instrument native to Appalachia but descended from the northern European zither. Another important instrument in Kentucky that developed in the Americas is the banjo, which is probably a combination of various instruments, including an African gourd instrument and the European mandolin.

The combination of British, country, folk, and slave songs led to the creation of an all-American form of music in Kentucky known as bluegrass. Bluegrass music is known throughout the world for its haunting melodies, beautiful lyrics, and often tragic love stories. Bill Monroe and the Blue Grass Boys were the first to popularize this traditional music, which uses the banjo, mandolin, fiddle, and other instruments. The headquarters of the International Bluegrass Music Association is in Owensboro, Kentucky.

One sport imported from Great Britain is foxhunting. At the state's major foxhunts, visitors love to watch the beautiful horses, packs of dogs, and riders dressed in bright colors. At these events, foxes are not killed, just chased. The foxhunt is mainly a chance for friends to ride their horses in the country and enjoy a traditional sport.

Foxhunters in Kentucky wear traditional English clothing and use English-style saddles and bridles.

MUSIC IN THEIR BLOOD

Bill Monroe, known as the Father of Bluegrass Music, was born near Rosine, Kentucky, and started playing the mandolin as a little boy. With his band, the Blue Grass Boys, he combined traditional mountain music with blues and gospel to form this new kind of music that was eventually called bluegrass after his group. When he debuted on the Grand Ole Opry, country music's most famous radio show, in 1939, the audience went wild after his first song, "Mule Skinner Blues." There was so much applause that he and his band had to do an encore—the first time this had happened in the program's ten-year history. Monroe was inducted into the Country Music Hall of Fame in 1970.

Loretta Lynn was the first woman ever to win the Country Music Association's Entertainer of the Year Award. Her autobiography, *Coal Miner's Daughter*, told about her life in Butcher Hollow, Kentucky, where she lived in poverty with her large and loving family. Loretta Lynn married at age thirteen and by age eighteen was the mother of four children. She often played guitar to her children and sang them lullabies. With her husband's encouragement, she started singing in restaurants and bars, which launched her career in country music. In 1980 *Coal Minter's Daughter* was made into a movie that brought country music to the attention of many Americans who until then had not listened to it.

Jean Ritchie also came from a large and loving family. The Ritchie family was so well known for singing traditional mountain songs that folk music collectors would often visit to hear them perform the old tunes. Many of these songs were traditional English ballads that Jean's great-grandfather had brought with him when he immigrated to America. Her family had learned other songs from neighbors. "Because we Ritchies loved to sing so well," she once said, "we always listened to people singing songs we didn't know, and

Bill Monroe (center) and his band the Blue Grass Boys were a popular musical group in Kentucky.

we caught many good ones that way." Jean, the youngest of fourteen children, started playing the dulcimer at age five. She grew up to be a teacher and a social worker, incorporating music in her work wherever she could. She eventually turned all of her attention to her true love and became a folk singer. In her long career she has made almost forty albums and has introduced American folk music to audiences the world over.

The mother-daughter singers Naomi and Wynonna Judd, who were both born in Ashland, Kentucky, always knew they had special talent. But like many people who want to be musicians, they had a hard time getting anybody to listen to them. Naomi was a nurse in Tennessee when they got their lucky break. The father of one of her patients worked in the record industry and arranged for them to have an audition with RCA Records in 1983. Almost immediately their sweet but strong voices and distinctive song styling made them stars. In addition to five Grammys, the Judds have won eight Country Music Association awards.

Wynonna (left) Naomi Judd perform in concert.

MAN O' WAR

Even people who know almost nothing about horses have heard of Man o' War. This chestnut Thoroughbred was born near Lexington in 1917. He was considered unbeatable, and in fact he lost only one race in his entire career. Once he won by an unbelievable one hundred times the length of a horse. As he won more and more races, his jockey was forced to carry handicap weights, intended to give the other horses a chance. They kept adding more and more weight until, in addition to the jockey, Man o' War was carrying 130 pounds in handicap weight.

His owner was once offered a million dollars for Man o' War, but he refused, saying, "Lots of men might have a million dollars, but only one man could have Man o' War." This magnificent horse, nicknamed Big Red, was so popular that when he died in 1947, more than one thousand people attended his funeral. He was buried at the Kentucky Horse Park in Louisville.

More than one million gather to celebrate at the Kentucky Derby Festival and Pegasus Parade (above).

Kentucky's real claim to fame is horse racing. The most famous horse race in the United States, the Kentucky Derby, has taken place at Louisville's Churchill Downs every May since 1875. Thousands of people watch the world's best three-year-old Thoroughbreds pound around the track each year.

But the Kentucky Derby isn't just a horse race. The whole city celebrates for two weeks before the race with the Kentucky Derby Festival. Over one million people attend this citywide party, enjoying the world's largest annual fireworks show, concerts, and, of course, many horse shows and exhibitions. "I love the Pegasus parade that goes along with the Derby festival," says Kentucky native Mary Anderson. "The horses are just beautiful. There is also a steamboat race and a balloon race."

Working or playing, Kentuckians have their own unique style. Twelve-year-old Jim Anderson says, "Kentucky is not what people think it is. It is a busy state." The Kentuckians who take pride in their state and their heritage have made it that way.

Chapter Four

Governing the Commonwealth

Kentucky's first government was established on June 4, 1792, when the commonwealth was formally separated from Virginia. Kentucky's legislative body, the General Assembly, first met a little over a year later in the newly established capital of Frankfort. One of the assembly's first acts was to start dividing Kentucky into many counties, some of them quite small. Today Kentucky has 120 counties, the second-highest number of counties per square mile in the United States (after Rhode Island).

INSIDE GOVERNMENT

Like the United States, Kentucky has three branches of government: executive, legislative, and judicial.

Executive

Kentucky's governor proposes the state budget to the legislature and signs bills into law. But the governor has less power than in some states.

The state capitol in Frankfort houses the official governmental offices, as well as the House of Representatives and the Senate.

For example, if the governor vetoes (refuses to sign) a bill, the legislature can vote on it again. If a majority is still in favor of the bill, the governor's veto is overridden and the bill becomes law. In most states it takes a two-thirds vote to override a veto. For most of Kentucky's history, a governor was limited to a four-year term. In 1999, thanks to an amendment to the state constitution, Paul Pattan became the first modern governor who could seek a second consecutive term.

Martha Layne Collins became Kentucky's first female governor in 1983. She had first entered the public eye as a teen when she was elected as Queen of the Kentucky Derby Festival. She was a junior high school teacher until she became involved in Democratic Party politics. As governor, she earned applause for reforming education and attracting new business to the state.

Kentucky's sixtieth governor, Ernie Fletcher, was elected in 2003, but came to office with experience from a variety of other careers. After serving in the U.S. Air Force as a fighter pilot, he went to medical school and then practiced medicine for twelve years. He has also served as a Baptist minister and as a representative in Kentucky's House of Representatives.

Legislative

The legislative branch is responsible for making the state laws. Kentucky's legislature, called the General Assembly, is made up of a senate with thirty-eight members and a house of representatives with one hundred members. Senators serve four-year terms, and representatives serve two-year terms.

Judicial

Most trials in Kentucky start out in circuit courts for serious offenses, or district courts for less serious offenses. If someone is dissatisfied with a verdict in a circuit or district court, he or she can ask a court of appeals to look at the case. The appeals court judges decide whether the original trial was conducted fairly.

Kentucky governor Ernie Fletcher says he is "working to increase opportunities for all Kentuckians . . . to generate economic growth and create jobs."

The highest court in Kentucky is the supreme court, which has seven justices, one from each region of the state. The supreme court decides whether rulings made by the lower courts are in line with the state constitution. It also reviews all trials that involve the death penalty or a prison sentence of more than twenty years. Supreme court justices are elected for eight-year terms; these terms never start at the same time, which prevents any group of judges from getting too much power.

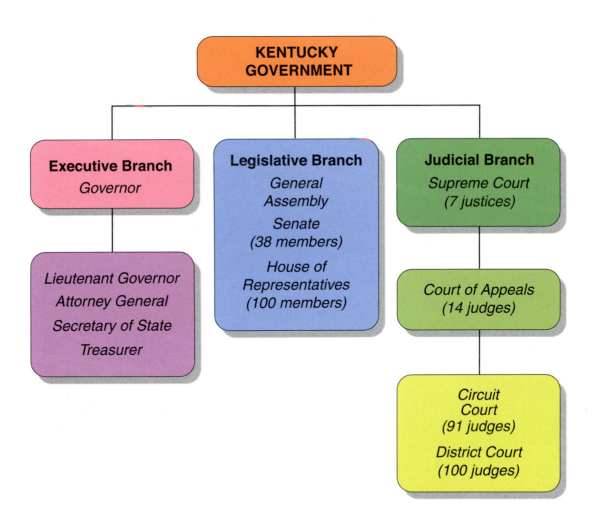

KENTUCKY GOVERNMENT

Executive Branch
Governor

Lieutenant Governor
Attorney General
Secretary of State
Treasurer

Legislative Branch
General Assembly
Senate (38 members)
House of Representatives (100 members)

Judicial Branch
Supreme Court (7 justices)

Court of Appeals (14 judges)

Circuit Court (91 judges)
District Court (100 judges)

BLOODY POLITICS

These days, Kentucky politics are relatively peaceful, but they haven't always been that way. Running for public office in the Bluegrass State used to be a hazardous business. For instance, a Democratic lawyer named William Goebel (below) was sworn in as governor in 1900. After a fierce campaign, Goebel appeared to have lost a close race to the Republican candidate, William S. Taylor. Although Goebel protested, Taylor was sworn in as governor. As an investigation of the election began, Goebel was shot as he walked toward the state capitol. The next day, the legislature, which was controlled by Democrats, declared that Goebel had actually won the election. Before Goebel died three days later, the Democrats swore him into office.

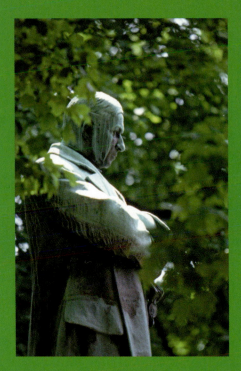

Some Democrats insisted that the Republicans had been behind Goebel's assassination. Taylor fled to Indiana, and his secretary of state and two other men were convicted of conspiracy to commit murder. Questions about what really happened persist to this day.

KENTUCKIANS IN PUBLIC SERVICE

Esteemed politician Henry Clay was known as the Great Compromiser for his skill in getting opponents to agree with each other. He started his political career in the Kentucky legislature in 1803, when he was just twenty-six years old. He later served in the U.S. Senate as the Speaker of the House of Representatives, and as secretary of state. Clay is perhaps best remembered for his efforts to avoid a civil war. He encouraged both the North and South to accept compromises that probably delayed the war. Although he lost all three of his campaigns for the presidency, Clay never abandoned his principles, saying, "I would rather be right than be president."

The twelfth president of the United States, Zachary Taylor, was born in Virginia. His family moved to Kentucky when he was only a few months old. Taylor grew up near Louisville, fought in the War of 1812, and was a hero in the Mexican War of the 1840s. His bravery earned him the nickname Old Rough and Ready. His "rough and ready" reputation didn't please everyone, however, including his political opponent Daniel Webster, who called him "a swearing, whiskey-drinking, fighting frontier colonel." Later, Webster grew to admire the president's decisive nature, saying, "I don't often agree with the man, but he does make decisions." Zachary Taylor fell sick early in his presidency and died in 1850, having served only a little more than one year in office.

After being admitted to the bar in 1797, Henry Clay began his legal career in Lexington, Kentucky.

Jefferson Davis, the first and only president of the Confederate States of America, was born near Elkton, Kentucky, and was the youngest of ten children. He attended the United States Military Academy at West Point and, like Zachary Taylor, was a hero of the Mexican War. He had a distinguished political career, serving in the U.S. Senate and as secretary of war. In 1844 a fellow politician described him as "the greatest man for soft words and hard arguments ever listened to."

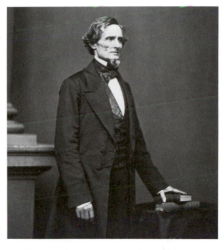

Jefferson Davis, president of the Confederate States of America, was born on June 3, 1808, in Todd County, Kentucky.

Davis's growing unhappiness with what he saw as the federal government's interference in individual states' affairs caused him to switch loyalties to the Confederacy, the group of states that seceded from the Union. In 1861 Davis became the president of the Confederate States of America. When the Confederacy lost the Civil War, Davis was captured by Union forces, and he spent two years in prison. After he was released, he traveled and eventually settled in Mississippi, where he spent the rest of his life.

Louis Brandeis, the first Jewish Supreme Court justice, was born in Louisville in 1856. He graduated from Harvard Law School at the age of twenty-two with the best grades in the school's history. He spent much of his legal career trying to help working people, fighting for low-cost life and health insurance, shorter workdays, and minimum-wage laws. He joined the Supreme Court in 1916 and continued working for social reform and human rights for another quarter century.

KENTUCKY BY COUNTY

MAKING THE GRADE

Kentuckians saw the importance of education from the beginning. Kentucky's Transylvania University, founded in 1780, was the first college west of the Allegheny Mountains.

Although Kentucky established public schools in 1849, the state was not wealthy and could not put much money into them. For more than one hundred years, education in Kentucky was worse than in most of the country. Miriam Moore, who attended public schools in rural Kentucky in the 1940s, recalls that some parents bitterly resented the government forcing their children to attend school when the parents wanted them to work in the fields. "Although the law said that they had to go, the officials kind of closed their eyes when parents kept their children at home. Once in a while, the

In 1940 these children attended a one-room schoolhouse in Breathitt County.

driver of the school bus would shout, 'Everybody down!' and we'd all have to lie on the floor. I didn't know it then, but what the bus driver was afraid of was someone shooting at him through the windows and hitting the kids." Moore says she was lucky to have a bus to take her to school. Two boys nearby had to travel on a mule. Miriam's school had no running water, and when a student had to visit the outhouse, the teacher would come along, carrying a gun. In this case the worry was not angry parents, but the wild boars that roamed the woods.

Becky Ray, who now holds a doctoral degree, grew up in central Kentucky in the 1950s and 1960s. She saw firsthand how difficult it was to get an education in the outskirts of the state. "Even though our school was only 10 miles away, it took us an hour and a half to get there on the bus," she says, "because there were so many kids living far apart for the bus driver to stop for." When Ray's family moved to the city, she quickly realized how sorely lacking her education had been. "We moved to Louisville when I was in high school," she recalls, "and the kids were complaining about having to write a paper. I was terrified—no one had ever even asked me to write a book report."

Finally, in 1988 sixty-four rural school districts sued the state government, saying that Kentucky had not lived up to its own constitution, which requires the state to have an efficient system of public schools. They argued that the rural schools were being neglected while those in the city were receiving far more than their fair share of financial support. The entire school system was declared unconstitutional, and the General Assembly passed the Education Reform Act in 1990 to improve the public schools. One of the act's most exciting innovations was to link smaller schools to larger ones by computer, so that a student in a small school could participate in classes in a city school hundreds of miles away. Improvements in education have been dramatic. In 1996 the National Education Association ranked Kentucky's schools among the top three of all fifty states.

Today, 74 percent of Kentuckians have graduated from high school—slightly below the national average, but an improvement over the statistics before the Education Reform Act. Seventeen percent of the state's citizens have a college degree.

Between 1998 and 2005 Kentucky's students have consistently ranked above the national average in reading and science and close to the average in mathematics and writing. Kentucky's Department of Education points out that "Kentucky's 4th-grade readers started out two points below the national average in 1992, equaled the national average in 1994, and moved three points above it in 1998. In 2005 the score was 220, three points higher than the national average."

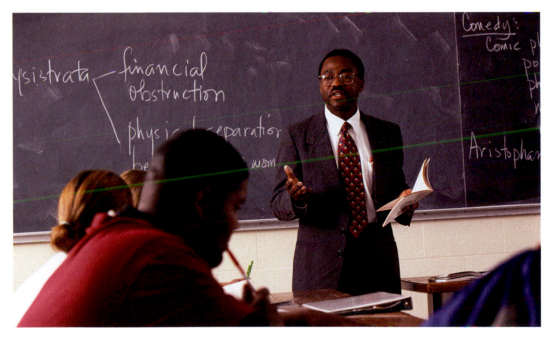

Kentucky continues to make strides in the education of its citizens.

Chapter Five

Kentucky at Work

Coal was first mined in Kentucky in 1790 and from that time until 2001 over 8 *billion* tons of coal have been dug up from the state's mines, almost 120 million tons from 432 mines in 2004 alone. Many Kentuckians have long depended on coal for their livelihood. But this has been a mixed blessing. Although the industry provides a great deal of employment, coal mining is not pleasant work. One miner said, "It's the worst job in the world. It's the dirtiest. It's the most unhealthy and the most dangerous. . . . It's always muddy and nasty and you wade in it and you lay down in it and you can't stand up till you come back out. It's just miserable." But with the lackluster state of education in Kentucky, until recently many workers were not qualified for other jobs.

Coal mining also harms Kentucky itself. It causes erosion, destroys forests, and pollutes the water. Since 1977 mining companies have been legally obligated to restore the land they damage, and many do. Unfortunately, some companies manage to dodge the law, leaving vast areas of ruined land behind them.

No matter their profession, Kentuckians work hard and take pride in their work.

Another problem with Kentucky's dependence on coal is that sometimes the demand for coal is low. When less coal is bought, coal companies close, and miners are out of work. This happened in the 1960s, and many Kentuckians left the state in search of other jobs. Then in the 1970s a worldwide shortage of oil made people turn back to coal as a source of energy. Kentuckians poured back into the state in what has been called "the greatest reverse migration in history." In 2004 Kentucky held third place in coal production of all the fifty states, after Wyoming and West Virginia.

In 2004 Kentucky produced 120 million tons of coal and employed over 15,000 people.

Agriculture is also important to Kentucky. Horses, cattle, and pigs are raised on ranches and farms throughout the state. Corn and soybeans are also important crops. Kentucky has more farms per square mile than any other state.

Kentucky's most valuable crop is tobacco. Kentucky produces more burley tobacco, a light-colored plant highly prized by cigarette manufacturers, than any other state. Not only do Kentuckians work in tobacco fields, but they also support this industry by their habits. In 2005, 27.5 percent of all Kentuckians smoked. Although this is a significant decrease from 30.5 percent in 2004, it is still the highest rate in the United States.

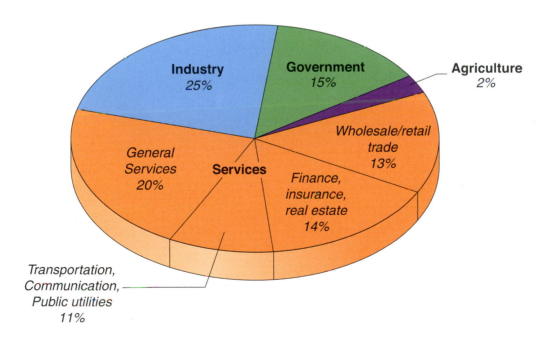

2005 GROSS STATE PRODUCT: $140 Million

Industry 25%
Government 15%
Agriculture 2%
Wholesale/retail trade 13%
General Services 20%
Services
Finance, insurance, real estate 14%
Transportation, Communication, Public utilities 11%

TOBACCO

Tobacco has a long history in Kentucky. Tobacco pipes four to five thousand years old have been found in the state. The plant was prized by many Native-American cultures. Some Native Americans used it in religious rituals or as medicine.

By the late 1700s the tobacco industry was established among Kentucky's white and black settlers. Louisville had factories that made cigars, pipe mixtures, snuff, and chewing tobacco.

Today, the future of tobacco in the state is uncertain. Because tobacco is dangerous to people's health, some politicians are trying to limit the amount grown. They also want to make cigarettes more expensive so people will not buy as many. Some farmers are turning to other crops so they won't be so dependent on tobacco for their income. Others worry that the increasing restrictions will ruin their livelihood. "I don't smoke, myself," says sixty-year-old tobacco farmer Jim Thornton, "but my family has owned this farm for four generations. I want my kids to inherit it, but it looks like they won't be able to. It's not good for growing anything but tobacco."

EARNING A LIVING

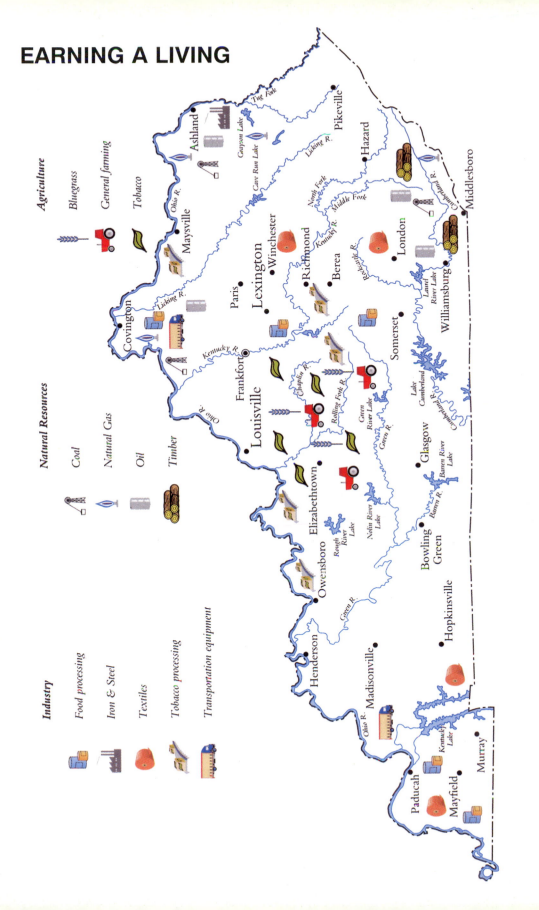

Agriculture

Bluegrass

General farming

Tobacco

Natural Resources

Coal

Natural Gas

Oil

Timber

Industry

Food processing

Iron & Steel

Textiles

Tobacco processing

Transportation equipment

Ashland

Pikeville

Hazard

Middlesboro

London

Williamsburg

Maysville

Winchester

Richmond

Berea

Covington

Paris

Lexington

Somerset

Frankfort

Louisville

Glasgow

Elizabethtown

Bowling Green

Owensboro

Hopkinsville

Henderson

Madisonville

Murray

Paducah

Mayfield

Tug Fork

Grayson Lake

Cave Run Lake

Licking R.

Ohio R.

Licking R.

Kentucky R.

North Fork

Middle Fork

Kentucky R.

Rockcastle R.

Cumberland R.

Laurel River Lake

Lake Cumberland

Cumberland R.

Green River Lake

Green R.

Barren River Lake

Barren R.

Chaplin R.

Rolling Fork R.

Nolin River Lake

Rough River

Green R.

Ohio R.

Kentucky Lake

Corn is another crop that has long been grown in Kentucky. Historically, most Kentucky corn was sold as animal feed, but the state's farmers sometimes grew so much that they couldn't sell it all. A few began making whiskey from the leftover grain, and Kentucky's bourbon industry was born. Some of the bourbon makers operated illegally and refused to pay alcohol taxes to the government. Since they often worked at night by the light of the moon to avoid detection, they became known as moonshiners, and their liquor was called moonshine. A few people still make moonshine, but it is not nearly as common as it was in the early 1900s. Kentucky's legal alcohol, especially its famous bourbon, remains an important industry in the state today.

Livestock also brings a lot of money into Kentucky. The state's hundreds of horse farms—where some of the world's greatest racehorses are born, raised, and trained—provide work for thousands of Kentuckians and draw a lot of tourists. Less visible but equally important to the economy is the beef cattle industry.

In Kentucky there are more than 110,000 dairy cows that yield $192 million in milk each year.

KENTUCKY WORKFORCE

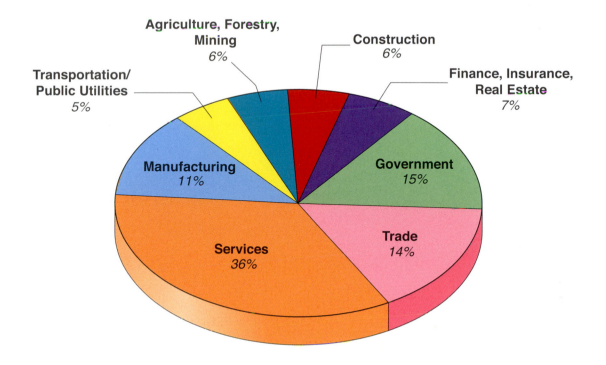

Agriculture, Forestry, Mining 6%

Construction 6%

Transportation/ Public Utilities 5%

Finance, Insurance, Real Estate 7%

Manufacturing 11%

Government 15%

Services 36%

Trade 14%

BUILDING THE FUTURE

Kentucky has long been one of the nation's poorest states. It ranks near the bottom in terms of personal income. Likewise, its poverty rate is higher than the national average. In 2005, 23.8 percent of the state's children lived in poverty, a jump from 18.1 percent in 2004 and among the worst rates in the nation. But Kentucky is working hard to improve its economy. Since World War II the state has attracted more and more manufacturing. Toyota Motor Manufacturing employs thousands of workers at its plant in Georgetown. Motor vehicles, railroad cars, chemicals, clothing, elevators, computers, and steel are all made in Kentucky.

Many major-league baseball players have their bats custom made at the Louisville Slugger factory.

The state has also been trying to help its economy by attracting more visitors. The amount of money brought in by tourists more than tripled during the 1990s. Today, about one-quarter of Kentucky's workers are in service jobs, which includes tourism.

Kentuckians have worked hard to improve the quality of life in their state, and their efforts show. Twelve-year-old Louisville native Jim Anderson said, "People should come here and see how great it is. They'd never want to leave."

Tourists visit the Kentucky Horse Park, which has exhibitions, a museum, and more than fifty breeds of horses for visitors to see.

Chapter Six

A Bluegrass Tour

No matter what kind of scenery you're looking for, Kentucky has it—except desert and seashore, that is. Beautiful mountains, rolling hills, fertile farmland, lakes, rivers, caves—you'll find it all in the Bluegrass State. Nearly 70 percent of the U.S. population can reach Kentucky in one day's drive, and many tourists take advantage of this easy access. Kentucky has encouraged tourism, building parks and attractions that are fun for everyone to visit. Their efforts have paid off. Today, tourism is thriving in Kentucky.

THE MOUNTAINOUS EAST

Most visitors to eastern Kentucky are drawn by natural wonders: the Appalachian Mountains, the caves, the rivers, and the beautiful parks. But don't leave eastern Kentucky without exploring its exciting cities and towns, too.

Historic Ashland is a great place to see centuries of Kentucky history all in one place. The families who began settling there in the eighteenth century built houses in the middle of ancient Native-American

The Kentucky Horse Park is located in the heart of the Bluegrass region.

burial mounds from two thousand years earlier. Today, visitors can tour the mounds, as well as many ornate eighteenth- and nineteenth-century homes. One such home even has two cast-iron dragons glaring down from its roof. The Kentucky Highlands Museum teaches visitors about the region's past, with exhibits on everything from the Adena culture to the development of radio. It also houses a great collection of antique clothing, as well as items owned by well-known country music artists.

The arts flourish in eastern Kentucky, particularly in Berea, which is known as Kentucky's crafts capital. The town is famous for its basket making, textiles, pottery, and woodworking. At Berea College, instructors keep old traditions alive while also teaching students modern styles.

Many people have seen a rainbow, but few have seen a "moonbow," unless they have traveled to eastern Kentucky's Cumberland Falls. When the conditions are just right, the light of the moon strikes the mist of the waterfall to create a moonbow. This wondrous phenomenon does not occur anywhere else in the Western Hemisphere.

Cumberland Falls is the second-largest waterfall east of the Rocky Mountains. It is 125 feet wide and falls 68 feet. Several well-marked trails give visitors spectacular views of the waterfall, which always has a rainbow arching out of it except on the cloudiest days. To give you a real feel for the power of the water, a guide will row you upriver to the very base of the falls. Everyone in the boat gets drenched by the pounding spray thrown up as the water hits the river, and conversation is impossible over the roar of the water.

Ian James, who pilots boats to the falls, is quick to point out the power of the water. "A few years ago," he recalls, "a man was out fishing and fell asleep in his boat. He woke up as it was going over the falls. He was pretty banged up, but he lived. A college girl who was wading and was swept away by the current wasn't so lucky."

Cumberland Falls is known as the Niagara of the South.

PLACES TO SEE

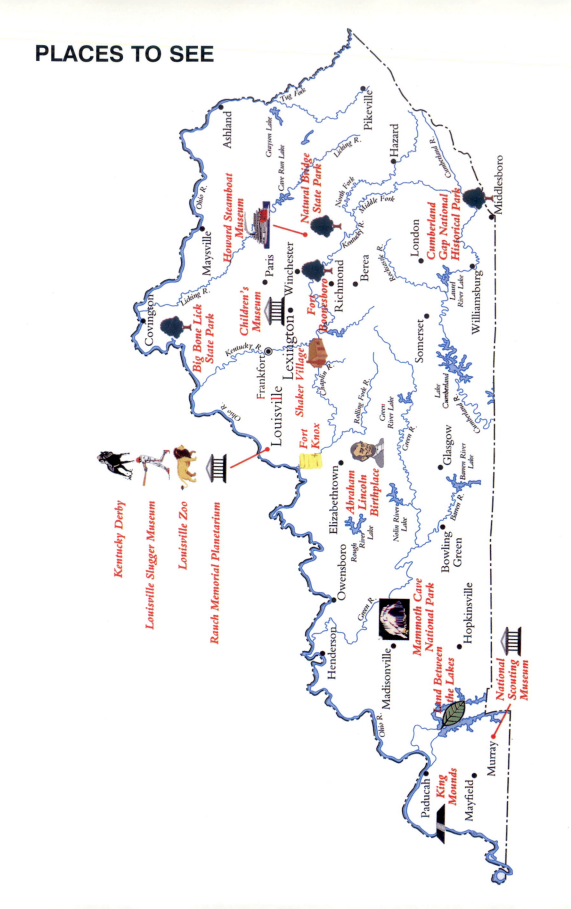

Ashland

Pikeville

Hazard

Middlesboro

Howard Steamboat Museum

Natural Bridge State Park

Grayson Lake

Cave Run Lake

Tug Fork

Ohio R.

Licking R.

Cumberland R.

North Fork

Middle Fork

Maysville

Paris

Winchester

Children's Museum

Fort Boonesboro

Richmond

Berea

London

Cumberland Gap National Historical Park

Williamsburg

Covington

Licking R.

Big Bone Lick State Park

Frankfort

Lexington

Fort Shaker Village

Kentucky R.

Kentucky R.

Rockcastle R.

Laurel River Lake

Somerset

Lake Cumberland

Cumberland R.

Kentucky Derby

Louisville Slugger Museum

Louisville Zoo

Rauch Memorial Planetarium

Louisville

Fort Knox

Chaplin R.

Rolling Fork R.

Green River Lake

Green R.

Glasgow

Barren River Lake

Barren R.

Elizabethtown

Abraham Lincoln Birthplace

Nolin River Lake

Rough River Lake

Owensboro

Green R.

Mammoth Cave National Park

Bowling Green

Hopkinsville

National Scouting Museum

Henderson

Madisonville

Ohio R.

Land Between the Lakes

Murray

King Mounds

Paducah

Mayfield

THE HEART OF KENTUCKY

You don't have to be a horse lover to enjoy the beautiful Bluegrass region; they say that if you don't love horses when you go to the Bluegrass, you will by the time you leave! But central Kentucky has more than Thoroughbreds. The world's largest cave system, exciting cities, beautiful rivers, and wonderful parks are all to be found in Kentucky's heartland.

Although not Kentucky's largest city, Lexington attracts the most visitors. Founded in 1775, Lexington was once known as the Athens of the West because of its wealth and many cultural attractions. The city is still a center of art and history. The Kentucky Gallery of Fine Crafts and Art showcases local craftspeople and artists, and the ArtsPlace Gallery also concentrates on Kentucky artists.

Not all of Lexington's museums are devoted to culture. The Explorium is one of the most visited children's museums in the country. The museum encourages visitors to touch, play, and explore with such displays as a giant human heart that you can walk through and a hands-on exhibit that shows how to create animation.

There's no doubt about it, horses are the major attraction of central Kentucky. And there's no better place for the horse lover than the Kentucky Horse Park. Located north of the city, the park is the Bluegrass region's most popular tourist attraction. People visit the park to see a huge statue of the most famous racehorse of all time, Man o' War, and to watch shows featuring more than forty breeds of horses. Special events are held throughout the year. For example, in the spring and summer, visitors are treated to the sight of newborn foals with their mothers. Knowledgeable guides talk about the special bonds between mothers and foals.

Man o' War is buried under a statue in his honor at the Kentucky Horse Park.

At the Kentucky Horse Park, the International Museum of the Horse provides much information for the curious. You can learn the history and characteristics of breeds, find out about the evolution of the horse from its earliest ancestors, and see examples of different sports involving horses. The Kentucky Horse Park is not just a spot to see horses—it is also a working thoroughbred training center where hundreds of animals are housed and trained.

The almost-vanished way of life of the Shaker community can be seen at the Shaker Village of Pleasant Hill just outside of Harrodsburg. This religious group was founded in 1805 and operated for about one hundred years. United by their belief in simple living and their devotion to God, community, and hard work, Shakers attempted to remove themselves from the rest of society and live in self-supporting communities. In the 1830s about five hundred Shakers lived and worked at Pleasant Hill. Shakers were renowned for their simple yet exquisite crafts. For instance, fabrics were sewn together so carefully that seams were hard to see. Today, you can tour Pleasant Hill's thirty-four buildings and watch craftspeople use traditional Shaker tools to demonstrate how Shakers made their beautiful furniture, brooms, and cloth.

The lifestyle of nineteenth-century Shakers is demonstrated at the Shaker Village in Pleasant Hill.

WORK IS WORSHIP

Shakers believed that work is worship, and that doing any less than their best when working was an insult to God. This accounts for their products' durability, as well as their practicality and beauty.

Shakers are credited with the invention of the flat broom. Before this invention, a broom was nothing but a tightly tied bundle of straw. The flat broom makes it easier to clean corners and is more durable than the earlier type of broom. Shakers were also the first to package seeds in envelopes, which were cheaper to manufacture and easier to ship than the boxes in which seeds had been sold earlier.

Shakers often made ingenious labor-saving devices. The houses at Pleasant Hill have many pegs on the walls. Everything that could be hung up was suspended from one of these pegs—when someone was finished with a chair, up it went on the wall (below). Brooms, ladders, and other tools had handles that could hook onto the pegs. Because everything was hung up, floors could be swept very quickly.

TEN LARGEST CITIES

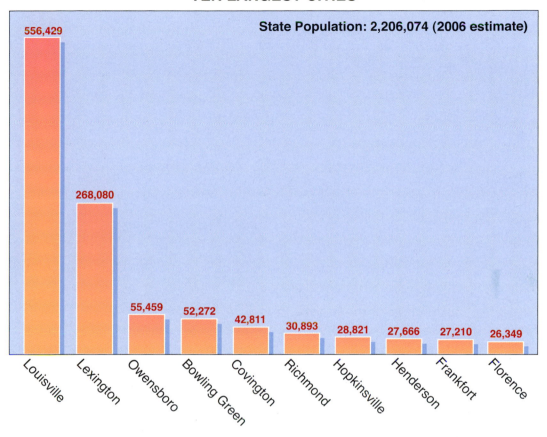

State Population: 2,206,074 (2006 estimate)

City	Population
Louisville	556,429
Lexington	268,080
Owensboro	55,459
Bowling Green	52,272
Covington	42,811
Richmond	30,893
Hopkinsville	28,821
Henderson	27,666
Frankfort	27,210
Florence	26,349

Kentucky's largest city, Louisville, is located in the central section of the state. The city was named for the French king Louis XVI in gratitude for his help to the young United States during the American Revolution. Although most famous as the site of the Kentucky Derby, Louisville is also rich in history and other attractions. Visitors can enjoy trips to the orchestra, opera, ballet, theater, and sporting events.

Louisville's early prosperity came from the Ohio River, and the river still plays an important role there. Visitors can view the city in one of the world's oldest operating steamboats, the *Belle of Louisville*.

The boat looks much the same today as it did when it began cruising the Ohio in 1914.

While horse fans know Louisville as the home of the Kentucky Derby, baseball fans have another association with the city: the Louisville Slugger, the most famous baseball bat in the world, is made there. The Louisville Slugger factory supplies 60 percent of all the baseball bats for professional teams in the United States. Many major league players travel to Louisville to personally pick out the wood that will be used for their bats, and to try out new shapes and sizes.

The Louisville Slugger Museum is a treasure trove for anyone who loves America's national sport. It is easy to spot—the world's largest bat looks like it's leaning on the building. This 120-foot-tall steel structure is supported only at its base and does not touch the building itself. "If there's ever a tornado, we're in trouble," jokes one of the tour guides. Rare and historic baseball memorabilia are on display there, and you can tour a locker room and a dugout. You can also see how baseball bats are made, starting in the forest and winding up at home plate.

South of Louisville is Fort Knox, where some of the gold belonging to the U.S. government is stored.

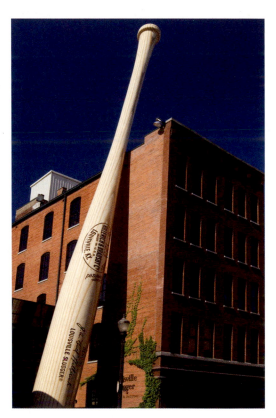

A giant baseball bat marks the spot of the Louisville Slugger Museum.

As you can imagine, security at Fort Knox is very strict. In fact, visitors are not even allowed. It is such a safe storage area that in addition to gold, other precious items have been stored there. During World War II original copies of the Declaration of Independence, the U.S. Constitution, and the Gettysburg Address were kept in vaults at Fort Knox. Although visitors are not permitted at the gold depository, Fort Knox welcomes everyone to tour its Patton Museum, which houses the U.S. Army's Museum of Cavalry and Armor.

One of the world's greatest natural wonders is in central Kentucky. Mammoth Cave is the longest known cave system in the world, with over 350 miles of mapped trails. Prehistoric people knew about this cave and mined minerals from it. Bodies of prehistoric people have been found in the cave, along with artifacts such as spearheads and sandals. The mummy of a woman buried in a stone coffin and wearing a necklace made of fawn hooves became a popular tourist attraction until her body was sent to the Smithsonian Institution in Washington. These peoples stopped using the cave about two thousand years ago. After it was rediscovered in the nineteenth century, the cave quickly became a fashionable spot to visit.

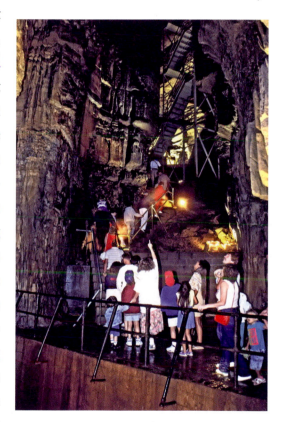

Visitors tour Mammoth Cave National Park, the longest cave system in the world.

Slaves would guide tourists through with lanterns and smoky torches. Today, the two million visitors who tour the cave each year can still see where some of these early tourists wrote their names on the ceiling with soot from the torches.

Because there is no light deep in the cave, strange animals have evolved in its depths. Eyeless fish, shrimp, and crayfish swim in the cave's pools, while eyeless beetles crawl along the walls and floors. Many of these animals have lost their coloration and look white or pink. These shy animals usually hide from visitors, but it is estimated that 130 species spend at least part of their lives in Mammoth Cave. Some have not been found anywhere else in the world.

Not far from Mammoth Cave, near Hodgenville, is the birthplace of President Abraham Lincoln. A log cabin similar to the one in which he was born sits on top of a hill near the stream where the Lincoln family got its water. Measuring only 12 by 17 feet, the modest cabin has only one door and one window. In the early nineteenth century, it was considered a good home.

WESTERN KENTUCKY

The long, narrow piece of land that is western Kentucky has some of the state's most beautiful wildlife. But don't forget to visit the many historic landmarks that are found there.

The great American art form, the patchwork quilt, has its most important museum in Paducah. Thousands of visitors come from all over the world to the Museum of the American Quilter's Society to admire these magnificent creations and to participate in the National Quilt Show. Patchwork quilts are made from small pieces of fabric sewn together in patterns and then attached to a backing by a pattern of stitches called quilting.

Most of the examples are considered works of art and are never used as bedspreads.

Land Between The Lakes National Recreation Area, on the border with Tennessee, opened in 1963. At the park, visitors learn about pre-Civil War farm life at the Homeplace, sixteen log buildings where early-nineteenth-century crafts are demonstrated.

Handcrafted quilts are on display at the Museum of the American Quilter's Society in Paducah.

Blacksmiths make horseshoes, people stir bubbling pots full of liquid soap, and whittlers carve charming figures out of wood. Rare and endangered animals can be seen at the park's Nature Station. But the park's most spectacular wild animals are the elk and bison that have been reintroduced into the area. Small herds of bison now roam the same fields where they were once plentiful.

Kentucky's wildlife has fascinated people for centuries. The illustrator John James Audubon lived in Henderson between 1810 and 1819, observing the birds that he would later gain fame for painting. The forest where he wandered has been turned into the John James Audubon State Park, which now contains a museum showing many of his lifelike paintings, as well as some of his journals and letters.

In 1924 humorist Irvin S. Cobb of Paducah said, "A Kentuckian stays put." Travel through the Bluegrass State, and you might be tempted to stay put, too.

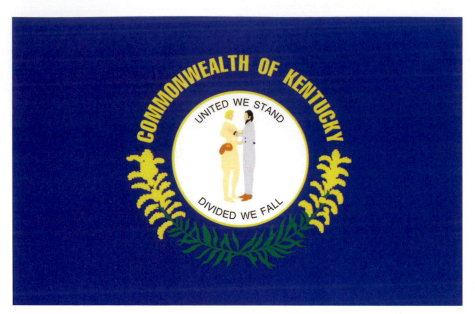

THE FLAG: *Adopted in 1918, the flag shows the state seal on a field of blue, surrounded by the words* Commonwealth of Kentucky *above and a wreath of goldenrod below.*

THE SEAL: *Adopted in 1792, the state seal depicts a frontiersman in buckskin shaking hands with a statesman dressed in a tailcoat. This symbolizes the relationship between Kentucky—the first "western" state—and its neighbors to the east. The two figures are encircled by the state motto, "United We Stand, Divided We Fall."*

State Survey

Statehood: June 1, 1792

Origin of Name: Probably derives from the Wyandot word *Kentahteh,* variously translated as "land of tomorrow," "land where we live," "meadow land," or "place of old fields." The name is also attributed to Iroquois and Wyandot words meaning "prairie," "meadow land," or "cane and turkey lands."

Nickname: Bluegrass State

Capital: Frankfort

Motto: United We Stand, Divided We Fall

Bird: Cardinal

Animal: Gray squirrel

Horse: Thoroughbred

Fish: Kentucky spotted bass

Insect: Viceroy butterfly

Flower: Goldenrod

Tree: Tulip poplar

Cardinal

Goldenrod

MY OLD KENTUCKY HOME

Since before the Civil War, the estate of Federal Hill, in Bardstown, has been known as the Old Kentucky Home. The name became attached to it because Stephen Foster may have composed the song "My Old Kentucky Home" there in 1850. In 1928 Foster's composition became the official state song.

GEOGRAPHY

Highest Point: 4,145 feet above sea level, at Black Mountain in Harlan County

Lowest Point: 257 feet above sea level, in southwestern Fulton County at the Mississippi River

Area: 39,732 square miles

Greatest Distance North to South: 180 miles

Greatest Distance East to West: 424 miles

Bordering States: Ohio, Indiana, and Illinois to the north; West Virginia and Virginia to the east; Tennessee to the south; and Missouri to the west

Hottest Recorded Temperature: 114 °F at Greensburg on July 28, 1930

Coldest Recorded Temperature: −37 °F at Shelbyville on January 19, 1994

Average Annual Precipitation: 48 inches

Major Rivers: Barren, Big Sandy, Cumberland, Dix, Green, Kentucky, Licking, Mississippi, Nolin, Ohio, Rockcastle, Rolling Fork, Salt, Tennessee, Tradewater, Tug

Major Lakes: Barkley, Barren, Buckhorn, Cave Run, Dewey, Fishtrap, Green, Herrington, Kentucky, Nolin, Reelfoot

Trees: ash, cypress, beech, buckeye, elm, hemlock, hickory, holly, linden, locust, maple, oak, pine, sassafras, sweet and black gum, sycamore, tulip poplar, walnut

Wild Plants: azalea, bloodroot, bluebell, bluegrass, buttercup, fringed gentian, ginseng, goldenrod, jack-in-the-pulpit, kudzu, mayapple, mountain laurel, pennyroyal, rhododendron, trillium, violet, watermeal

Animals: black bear, fox, mink, mouse, opossum, raccoon, river otter, shrew, skunk, squirrel, white-tailed deer

Birds: bald eagle, blue jay, brown thrasher, cardinal, catbird, chickadee, crested flycatcher, dove, duck, goose, grouse, hawk, osprey, owl, robin, slate-colored junco, sparrow, starling, towhee, tufted titmouse, wild turkey, yellow-bellied sapsucker

Fish: bass, bluegill, catfish, crappie, drum, jack salmon, rainbow trout, sauger, sucker, walleye, white perch

Endangered Animals: American peregrine falcon, bald eagle, blackside dace, clubshell, fanshell, fat pocketbook, gray bat, Indiana bat, Kentucky cave shrimp, least tern, northern riffleshell, palezone shiner, pallid sturgeon, pearly mussel, pink ring mussel, piping plover, red-cockaded woodpecker, relict darter, tan riffleshell, Virginia big-eared bat, winged mapleleaf mussel

Peregrine falcon

Endangered Plants: Cumberland rosemary, Cumberland sandwort, Price's potato-bean, running buffalo clover, Short's goldenrod, Virginia spiraea, white-haired goldenrod

TIMELINE

Kentucky History

1600s The Cherokee, Chickasaw, Wyandot, Delaware, and Shawnee tribes use the region as a hunting ground.

1750 Dr. Thomas Walker becomes the first European known to have come through the Cumberland Gap, which he names.

1767 Daniel Boone enters and explores the region.

1774 Virginia defeats the Cherokee, Chickasaw, Wyandot, Delaware, and Shawnee tribes and forces them to sign a treaty giving up all rights to lands south of the Ohio River.

1774 James Harrod founds Kentucky's first permanent settlement.

1775 Daniel Boone establishes Fort Boonesborough on the south bank of the Kentucky River.

1776 Kentucky officially becomes the region's name when it becomes a county of Virginia.

1778–1779 During the American Revolution General George Rogers Clark defeats Indian, French, and British forces at Vincennes in Indiana.

1782 Indians defeat settlers at Blue Licks, the last major Indian battle in the region.

1792 Kentucky becomes the fifteenth state.

1809 Abraham Lincoln is born on February 12 in a log cabin near Hodgenville.

1849 Kentuckian Zachary Taylor becomes the twelfth president of the United States.

1861 State is deeply divided by the Civil War; more than 90,000 men enlist with the Union forces and 35,000 men with the Confederates.

1865–1870 Following the Civil War, industry thrives but many farmers are bankrupted by financial panics.

1875 First Kentucky Derby is run at Churchill Downs.

1891 Fourth and present state constitution is adopted.

1899–1900 During a contested election for governor, the declared winner, William Goebel, is shot and killed. His successor and opponent vie for power, which almost erupts into a civil war.

1905–1909 During the so-called Black Patch War, bands of night-riding terrorists in western Kentucky try to force tobacco farmers into joining cooperatives.

1930s Many strikes in the coal fields erupt in violence between strikers and armed guards hired by the coal companies; the Great Depression drives many farmers off their land to seek employment in urban areas.

1941–1945 World War II brings a boom to the state's mining and manufacturing industries, as factories produce war materials.

1950s Opening of interstate highways and four-lane toll roads connects isolated sections of the state.

1954 The public school system is desegregated.

1960s Kentucky passes strict laws requiring mining companies to restore and reforest strip mine pits.

1964 Kentuckian Muhammad Ali (born Cassius Clay) becomes the boxing World Heavyweight Champion.

1966 Kentucky is the first southern state to pass a comprehensive civil rights law.

1970 Majority of the state population is urban rather than rural for the first time.

1983 Martha Layne Collins is elected the state's first female governor.

1987 Toyota builds a giant automobile manufacturing plant near Georgetown, bringing jobs and satellite industries to the state.

1990 State supreme court declares the state's public school system is unconstitutional and orders the General Assembly to create a new system which distributes educational funds fairly between rural and urban districts.

1996 National Education Association rates Kentucky's schools among the top three in the nation.

1997 Student Michael Carneal opens fire at Heath High School in McCracken County, killing three students and wounding five others.

2000 State pledge of allegiance is adopted: "I pledge allegiance to the Kentucky flag, and to the Sovereign State for which it stands, one Commonwealth, blessed with diversity, natural wealth, beauty, and grace from on High."

2006 An airplane crashes shortly after takeoff at Lexington's Bluegrass Airport, killing forty-nine of fifty passengers aboard; five miners are killed in an explosion in a coal mine in Harlan County.

ECONOMY

Agricultural Products: beef cattle, corn, forest products, hay, horses, poultry, silk, soybeans, tobacco

Tobacco

Manufactured Products: automobiles, chemicals, electronics, food processing, metalworking, petrochemicals, pottery and glass products, textiles, tobacco products, transportation equipment, whiskey

Natural Resources: coal, natural gas, oil, stone

Business and Trade: construction, finance, insurance, printing and publishing, real estate, tourism, transportation

CALENDAR OF CELEBRATIONS

Humana Festival of New American Plays From late February through April in Louisville, this renowned festival offers you a chance to see world premieres of new plays. In past years the festival has featured plays by such internationally recognized writers as Beth Henley, John Guare, Athol Fugard, Wole Soyinka, Jimmy Breslin, Harry Crew, Marsha Norman, Arthur Kopit, Joyce Carol Oates, Lanford Wilson, and Tony Kushner.

The Paducah Dogwood Trail Celebration Each April visitors to Paducah are invited to travel a 12-mile trail to admire the blooms of these beautiful flowering trees.

Kentucky Derby The Derby started in 1875. Since 1938 the "Run for the Roses" has been held on the first Saturday in May when huge crowds turn out to cheer on their favorite horses and jockeys at this internationally famous horse race at Churchill Downs in Louisville.

Kentucky Derby

The Mountain Laurel Festival Pine Mountain State Resort Park near Pineville hosts this annual mid-May festival. Visitors can admire the laurel blossoms as they walk the park's nature trails, then linger to browse and buy mountain handicrafts on display by local artists and craftspeople.

Highland Games At the end of May and beginning of June this festival of Scottish traditions at Glasgow features athletic events, such as the caber toss and the stone throw, plus traditional and contemporary Scottish music.

Boone Day Every June, the anniversary of the month Daniel Boone first entered Kentucky, the Kentucky Historical Society commemorates Boone Day with such activities as historical reenactments, lectures, and genealogy workshops.

Official Kentucky State Championship Old-Time Fiddlers Contest Audiences will have trouble keeping their toes from tapping as the best musicians from around the country compete in fifteen categories of old-time and bluegrass fiddle music the third Friday and Saturday of every July in Falls of Rough.

Kentucky State Fair More than 600,000 people turn out each August at the Kentucky Fair and Exploration Center in Louisville for such events as horse shows, cooking contests, education programs, carnival rides, and performances by top-name music acts.

Bluegrass Music Festival of the United States Visitors can bring their dancing shoes or just relax in the sun on Labor Day weekend as Louisville celebrates the state's own homegrown brand of music with one of the largest free bluegrass music events in the country. Hear the best performers in the country on the guitar, banjo, dulcimer, fiddle, mandolin, and autoharp.

Festival of the Horse This annual October event in Georgetown features exhibits involving everything imaginable relating to horses, plus arts and crafts and music.

Trail of Tears Indian Powwow This Native-American gathering each October in Hopkinsville commemorates the 1838 forced removal of the Cherokees from their lands to reservations in Oklahoma. Everyone is welcome at this giant display of Native-American dancing, crafts, and storytelling.

North American International Livestock Exposition Those who travel to Louisville in November can see hordes of handsome cattle, horses, swine, sheep, and goats at one of the largest livestock shows in the world. More than $5 million in prizes is awarded every year.

North American Championship Rodeo Every February real cowboys show what they can do as Bowling Green hosts the top twenty rodeo competitors in the world in seven events, including cattle roping and branding, bucking broncos, and fancy horseback riding.

Bluegrass Music Festival of the United States

My Old Kentucky Home Candlelight Tours During this tour visitors can view nineteenth-century holiday decorations—Yule logs, candlelit trees, paper angels, and homemade candies—as musicians and carolers entertain in November and December in this famous Bardstown home.

Appalachian Christmas Arts and Crafts Market Artists and craftspeople display their quilts, crockery, carvings, embroidery, knitting, musical instruments, paintings, and drawings in Morehead during December.

The Shaker Order of Christmas Shaker holiday traditions and music are on display at Pleasant Hill during December, when people can hear—and dance to—Shaker hymns, and also sample the simple, rich, and delicious Shaker cooking.

STATE STARS

Muhammad Ali (1942–   ) was born Cassius Clay in Louisville. He was the gold medal winner in boxing at the 1960 Olympics and became the boxing World Heavyweight Champion in 1964. The title was taken from him in 1967 when he was convicted of draft evasion for refusing to serve in the army for religious reasons. Following a Supreme Court ruling that overturned his conviction, Ali regained his title in 1974. Ali's engaging personality and passionate involvement in the civil rights movement brought him fame outside the ring. Although he retired from boxing in 1981, he remains one of the world's most popular sports figures.

Muhammad Ali

Henry Clay (1777–1852) was born in Virginia but settled in Kentucky in 1797. As a U.S. senator he was known as the Great Compromiser for his work on the Missouri Compromise. He was secretary of state under President John Quincy Adams and served in the U.S. Senate on three separate occasions.

George Clooney (1961–   ) is a popular actor who rose to fame playing a doctor in the television show *ER*. He has starred in, directed, and produced many films, being the only person ever nominated for two Academy Awards in the same year (2005) for acting in one film and directing another.

John Colgan (1840–1916), a druggist from Louisville, was the inventor of the first chewing gum, Colgan's Taffy Tolu, which gained widespread popularity after it was introduced at the 1893 World's Columbia Exposition (Chicago).

Martha Layne Collins (1936–   ) was the first female governor of Kentucky, serving from 1983 through 1987. Born in Shelby County, she first attracted public attention as a teen when she was selected as Queen of the Kentucky Derby Festival. Before becoming involved in politics, she was a junior high school teacher. As governor, Collins was noted for her reform of the state's educational system and for attracting new businesses to the state. She later served as a college president of Saint Catharine College.

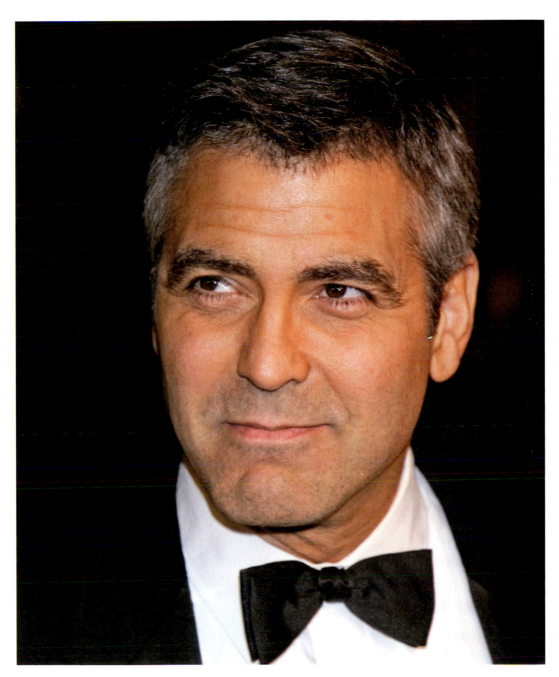

George Clooney

Ashley Judd (1968–), born Ashley Tyler Ciminella in California, was raised in Kentucky along with her half-sister Wynonna by their mother Naomi Judd. She has had a successful career as an actor on television and in films, and as a model and spokesperson for Estée Lauder cosmetics.

Naomi (1946–) and **Wynonna** (1964–) **Judd** were both born in Ashland. As the popular mother-daughter singing duo, the Judds, they won the Country Music Association Award for Vocal Group of the Year every year from 1985 through 1992. In 1993, after health problems stopped Naomi from performing, Wynonna went solo and won the Best Female Vocalist of the Year Award. Among the Judds' hits are "She Is His Only Need," "I Saw the Light," "My Strongest Weakness," and "Love Can Build a Bridge."

Barbara Kingsolver (1955–) was raised in Carlisle. Her nonfiction, poetry, prose poems, and novels have won many awards. *The Poisonwood Bible* was a finalist for a Pulitzer Prize and a PEN/Faulkner Award and was an Oprah's Book Club selection. In 2000 President Bill Clinton awarded Kingsolver the National Humanities Medal.

Abraham Lincoln (1809–1865), the sixteenth president of the United States, was born in a log cabin on his father's homestead near Hodgenville. His family moved to Indiana when he was seven and to Illinois when he was twenty-one. His early education was slight; as an adult he estimated that his total formal schooling amounted to less than one year. Nevertheless, Lincoln became a lawyer. After serving in

Ashley Judd

the Illinois legislature and the U.S. House of Representatives, in 1860 he was elected president. He led the nation through the Civil War but was assassinated shortly after the war ended.

Loretta Lynn (1935–) has had a long career as one of the most popular female country music singers in the nation. Lynn was born into a poor coal miner's family in Butcher Hollow. Her autobiography, *Coal Miner's Daughter*, was made into a very successful movie. Among her best-known songs are "You Ain't Woman Enough," "Don't Come Home a' Drinkin'," and "Coal Miner's Daughter."

Bobbie Ann Mason (1940–), born in Mayfield, is a novelist and short story writer best known for her novels *In Country*, *Feather Crowns*, and *Spence and Lila*. Her short story collection *Shiloh and Other Stories* won the Ernest Hemingway Award in 1983. *In Country* was made into a movie in 1989.

Thomas Merton (1915–1968) was a Trappist monk and a widely published writer and poet who spent most of his adult life at the monastery at Gethsemani, Kentucky. His early autobiography, *The Seven Storey Mountain*, was a national best seller. More than forty books followed on the subjects of peace, poverty, and social justice.

Bill Monroe (1911–1996), known as the Father of Bluegrass Music, was born on a farm just outside of Rosine. Monroe combined traditional Appalachian music with gospel and blues to create a new type of music, which came to be called bluegrass after his band, the Blue Grass Boys. In 1970 Monroe was inducted into the Country Music

Loretta Lynn

Diane Sawyer (1945–), a nationally recognized television news journalist, was born in Glasgow. Sawyer was the first female reporter on the CBS news program *60 Minutes*. Currently, she is the host of ABC's *Good Morning America*.

Ricky Skaggs (1954–), an internationally known country and bluegrass artist, was born in Lawrence County. He joined the Grand Ole Opry in 1982 and has won numerous Grammy and Country Music Association awards.

Phillip A. Sharp (1944–) won the Nobel Prize in medicine and physiology in 1993 for the discovery of split genes and for advancing research on cancer and hereditary diseases. Born in Falmouth, he has said that his childhood "in the northern hill country of Kentucky" was important in shaping his life.

Jesse Hilton Stuart (1906–1984), a popular author, was famous for his novels, short stories, and poems featuring his beloved Kentucky hill country. In 1980 the former schoolteacher donated 700 acres of land, which his parents had worked as tenant farmers, to the state as a nature preserve.

Zachary Taylor (1784–1850), the twelfth president of the United States, grew up in Jefferson County. He served with distinction in the War of 1812 and became a national hero for his successful conduct of the Mexican War. He became president in 1849 but died after only serving sixteen months in office.

Diane Sawyer

Kentucky Horse Park (Lexington) This thousand-acre park includes the International Museum of the Horse, which documents the history of all breeds of horses.

Mary Todd Lincoln House (Lexington) The girlhood home of Abraham Lincoln's wife is a restored house from 1803 containing period furniture and decorations from the Lincoln and Todd families.

Explorium (Lexington) This museum is the place for active, inquisitive kids. It features hands-on exhibits about science, nature, history, and ecology.

Nostalgia Station Toy and Train Museum (Versailles) A restored 1911 railroad station houses a model train display that is a treat for children of all ages. Exhibits include complete Lionel train layouts from 1926 and the 1960s with all the original accessories, as well as numerous children's toys and railroad memorabilia.

Shaker Village (Pleasant Hill) This restored Shaker village, which was founded in 1806, is the largest in the United States. The site contains many of the original living quarters, barns, and workshops.

Old Fort Harrod State Park (Harrodsburg) The park is on the land originally colonized by Captain James Harrod in 1774. From March to October, costumed staff portray the lives of the residents of the first permanent English settlement west of the Alleghenies.

Explorium

ABOUT THE AUTHOR

Tracy Barrett is the author of numerous fiction and nonfiction books for young readers. Tracy holds an A.B. from Brown University and an M.A. and Ph.D. from the University of California at Berkeley. She is married and has two grown children. She lives in Nashville, Tennessee, where she teaches at Vanderbilt University. She is the Regional Advisor for the Midsouth of the Society of Children's Book Writers and Illustrators. Visit her at www.tracybarrett.com.